METR1C SYSTEM SIMPLIFIED

REVISED AND ENLARGED EDITION

By Gerard W. Kelly

STERLING PUBLISHING CO., INC. NEW YORK

Oak Tree Press Co., Ltd. London & Sydney

A Worm's Quandary

What will the careful inchworm do,
Will calculation quite defeat her,
When she must soon, as we must too,
Convert from inch to centimeter?

Will she persist in inching still,
Although it will become archaic,
Could centimetering fulfill
Her, when its sound is so prosaic?

P. Brown

27360

Ninth Printing, 1978

Revised Edition

Copyright © 1976, 1974, 1973 by Gerard W. Kelly

Published by Sterling Publishing Co., Inc. .
Two Park Avenue, New York, N.Y. 10016
Distributed in Australia by Oak Tree Press Co., Ltd.,
P.O. Box J34, Brickfield Hill, Sydney 2000, N.S.W.
Distributed in the United Kingdom
by Ward Lock Ltd., 116 Baker Street, London W.1
Manufactured in the United States of America
All rights reserved
Library of Congress Catalog Card No.: 72–95207
Sterling ISBN 0-8069- 3058–6 Trade   Oak Tree 7061- 2438 –3
3059–4 Library

CONTENTS

About This Book 4

Introduction 5

I. The United States System of Weights and Measures 13

II. The Metric System of Weights and Measures 17

III. Going from the U.S. to the Metric System . 32

IV. Converting to Metric for Everyday Use . . 46

V. Conversions Between Fahrenheit and Celsius (Centigrade) Temperatures 57

VI. Metric in the Kitchen 61

VII. Metric and the Car 67

VIII. Short-Cut Conversions from U.S. to Metric 72

IX. Working with Metric Measurements . . . 76

X. Simple Science in Metric 83

Additional Tables 92

Index 95

List of Tables 96

ABOUT THIS BOOK

This is a ready-reference book on the metric system of weights and measures. It tells how the metric system was developed, how it is organized, and how it can be applied in various fields. It shows also how the metric system is related to our U.S. customary system.

The book explains how to change quickly and easily from one U.S. unit to another, from one metric unit to another, from the U.S. system to metric, and from metric to U.S. units. It includes a variety of methods, tables, formulas, and short-cuts that have been developed and simplified especially for this book.

The information can be used to advantage anywhere —in school, at home, in an office or shop, on the farm, on the job, in a science laboratory, or while travelling in a metric country. Anyone able to do simple arithmetic can understand and apply the metric system as it is simplified in this book.

How you use the book will depend, of course, upon your own needs—upon whether you are a student, a homemaker, a businessman, a mechanic, a farmer, or someone else. You might want to use it as a handbook for general reference, as an aid in preparing to "live and think" in metric, or for help in converting between U.S. and metric units as the need arises.

To get the most out of the book, read through it briefly to see what is in it and how it is organized. Make a note of items of special interest that you may wish to study further. Keep the book handy for reference and browse through it from time to time as a refresher or for general review.

4

INTRODUCTION

1. Early Measurement Units

Man's early units of measurement were based on parts of the human body. The ancient "cubit," for example, was the length of the forearm from the elbow to the tip of the middle finger (about 18 to 22 inches), and a "palm" was the width of four fingers.

A man's foot was another early unit and varied from 10 to 13 inches, depending upon whose foot was being used. These early units were not very precise, of course, but they were always available and easy to use.

The Romans divided their foot into 12 unciae or inches. They also called two steps of a soldier a passus or pace, and made 1,000 paces a mile (from the Latin "mille," meaning a thousand). As the Romans marched all over Europe, they brought their inch, foot, and mile with them, and these became common units of length in European countries.

In these early days, too, stones were used as units of weight. Within a given town or area, the stones would weigh about the same and provide a workable "standard," but their weight differed from town to town so that throughout Europe stones varied from 4 to 26 pounds.

2. The English System of Weights and Measures

In the twelfth century, England's Henry I defined the yard as the distance from his nose to the end of his thumb with his arm extended sideways. The inch was originally the width of a man's thumb but was later defined as the length of three grains of barley placed end to end.

Seeds of grain (wheat, rice, and barley) were used as an early English unit of weight. In the sixteenth century, Henry VIII decreed the pound to be 7,000 grains of wheat, and there are still 7,000 "grains" to the pound (avoirdupois).

The English kept improving the accuracy of their standards and units of measurement so that, long before America was colonized, the English system of weights and measures had become the best standardized and most widely used in the world. It was this system that the English colonists brought to America with them and which became the system of weights and measures commonly used in the States.

Although the system of weights and measures used in the United States was inherited from the English, the system is now somewhat different and is known as the U.S. customary system, or simply the U.S. system, as it is called in this book.

In 1965, the British government decided to adopt metric as the legal system of measurement in the United Kingdom and planned to complete its "metrication" program by 1975.

3. The Metric System of Weights and Measures

A plan for a metric system was first proposed by Gabriel Mouton in France in 1670. A decimal system that would use a measurement of the earth to provide a fixed standard, it was intended to eliminate the confusion of weights and measures that made it so difficult for merchants to carry on trade and for scientists to compare their measurements. Mouton's idea was to establish a single, unchanging system that could be used throughout the world for all measuring needs—commercial as well as scientific.

The idea was debated for more than a hundred years. Then, in 1790, the French Academy of Sciences undertook to "deduce an invariable standard for all measures and weights." The result was the metric system. Although the metric standards were ready in 1799, their adoption was slow because of political obstacles and the natural inclination of people to keep using their old familiar units.

Finally, the French Parliament passed a law that only the metric system could be used for public commerce in France after January 1, 1840. Today, metric is the international measuring system of science and the commercial system of weights and measures in most countries.

The basic unit of length, the "meter," was originally intended to be 1/10,000,000 of the distance from the north pole to the equator on a line running through Paris. However, errors were found in these calculations and the meter was later defined as the distance between two lines marked on a platinum-iridium bar especially constructed for this purpose. A platinum-iridium weight was also constructed, equal to the mass of 1 kilogram. This standard meter and standard kilogram are kept at the International Bureau of Weights and Measures in Sèvres, near Paris.

Since its beginning, the metric system has undergone many revisions. In 1960, by international agreement, the system was extensively revised and simplified to produce the modern International System of Units. The standard of mass is still the platinum-iridium kilogram weight mentioned above but the meter is now defined in terms of the wavelength of the orange-red radiation of krypton-86 (a gas). With this new standard, measurements can be made to the nearest 0.000 000 01 inch. Such high precision is important in the guidance systems of space rockets.

Besides the units of length and mass, the modern metric system defines other base units, such as for temperature, time, electric current, and luminous intensity, but some of these are too special to be discussed in this book.

4. How the U.S. and Metric Systems Are Related

Use of the metric system of weights and measures in the United States was authorized by Act of Congress on July 28, 1866. This made it legal to use the metric system but did not compel its use so that the customary and metric systems continued to exist side by side.

In 1875, the United States joined other powers in establishing the International Bureau of Weights and Measures, and in 1890 received exact copies of the standard meter and kilogram. In 1893, these were declared to be the fundamental standards of length and mass, and since then U.S. units of measurement have been based on standard metric units. The yard is legally defined as 0.9144 meter and the pound as 0.45359237 kilogram. All other U.S. units of weights and measures are derived from these fundamental units.

Metric has long been put to practical use in the U.S. It is the measurement language of science—the same as used by scientists throughout the world. Doctors write prescriptions in metric units and pharmacists fill them in metric, too. The metric system is being taught in mathematics and science education, even to very young children.

U.S. coins are made to metric standards. The 1971 half dollar, for example, weighs 11.34 grams and has a diameter of 30.6 millimeters. Diamonds are weighed in metric, with 200 milligrams to the carat.

The Army measures its weapons in millimeters. The electric company charges by the kilowatt-hour. Tools come in metric sizes for automotive mechanics. Distances of many sports events are given in meters and kilometers. Photographic film comes in the familiar 8-, 16-, and 35-millimeter sizes. Food packages often show the contents in metric as well as in U.S. units. Many other examples could be cited.

Then, in 1971, when the National Bureau of Standards completed its report on the U.S. Metric Study, the Department of Commerce recommended to Congress that "the United States should change to the metric system through a coordinated national program."

5. "Going Metric" on a National Basis

Experience has shown that when a country "goes metric" on a national basis, it takes *time* to change.

People need time to learn the metric system—to use the metric language—to become accustomed to "thinking metric." It takes time to stop using the customary measuring units and devices—time to manufacture metric tape measures, measuring cups, weighing scales, and so on. It takes time to get the new metric devices distributed and into common use.

It takes time for metric to be taught in schools as the national measurement system—time to plan the courses and to prepare the books and other educational aids. It takes time to inform and educate the public. Businesses and industries need time to convert to metric and to train their employees. It takes time for food packages to be changed and for consumers to get used to the new weights and measures. And so it goes.

However, in countries that have gone metric, the changeover was usually easier than had been expected. People were often surprised at how easy it was to learn metric—to live and work with metric measurement—within a reasonable amount of time.

During a changeover from customary to metric units, people need to talk in two measurement languages and must therefore be able to "translate" or convert from one to the other. This period of transition will last longer for some than for others, depending upon how much and what kind of measuring they must do, but eventually all—or almost all—will learn to use metric as their basic measurement language. In time, many of the old customary units will disappear like the "cubit" of old.

6. "Going Metric" on a Personal Basis

How much metric *you* will need depends upon how much measuring *you* must do and how important measurement is in *your* life. An engineer, a student, a housewife, and a carpenter will obviously have different requirements. The sensible approach is to learn only the metric you need and can put to practical use. This is the metric that will benefit *you*—it's the metric you will *want* to learn—and wanting to learn gets you off to a good start; in fact, it puts you half way there.

Children who are taught the metric system as their primary measurement language learn to "think metric" from the beginning. But people "brought up" on the customary system face a different situation. Besides learning the metric units, they must also learn to let go of the old system and to think in the new. Some, especially of the older generation, will be unable or unwilling to do this. And so we will probably have to be "bi-lingual"—able to speak and understand both measurement languages—until the old units fade away.

To "think metric" is generally recommended as the best way to learn metric. This sums it up nicely in two words, but while you're thinking about it, be sure to also "measure in metric," "apply metric," "live metric," and "work with metric." It's the way we learn just about anything.

TABLE 1-1: U.S. SYSTEM OF WEIGHTS AND MEASURES

LENGTH
(linear measure)

12 inches (in.)	= 1 foot (ft.)
3 feet	= 1 yard (yd.)
16½ feet (5½ yd.)	= 1 rod (rd.)
40 rods (660 ft., or 220 yd.)	= 1 furlong (fur.)
5,280 feet (1,760 yd.)	= 1 statute or land mile (mi.)
8 furlongs	= 1 mile

AREA
(square measure)

144 square inches (sq. in.)	= 1 square foot (sq. ft.)
9 square feet	= 1 square yard (sq. yd.) (= 1,296 sq. in.)
30¼ square yards	= 1 square rod (sq. rd.)
160 square rods	= 1 acre (a.) (= 43,560 sq. ft., or 4,840 sq. yd.)
640 acres	= 1 square mile (sq. mi.)

VOLUME
(cubic measure)

1,728 cubic inches (cu. in.)	= 1 cubic foot (cu. ft.)
27 cubic feet	= 1 cubic yard (cu. yd.)

CAPACITY
Dry Measure

2 pints (pt.)	= 1 quart (qt.) (67.2 cu. in.)
8 quarts	= 1 peck (pk.) (537.61 cu. in.)
4 pecks	= 1 bushel (bu.) (2,150.42 cu. in., or 1.244 cu. ft.)

(Continued on page 14)

I. THE UNITED STATES SYSTEM OF WEIGHTS AND MEASURES

The U.S. system of weights and measures is given here to provide a ready reference for the units used in every-day life, a review of the methods by which U.S. units are changed from one to another, and a basis for comparing the U.S. and metric systems.

1-1. Units in the U.S. System of Weights and Measures

The system of weights and measures commonly used in the United States is shown in Table 1-1. The numbers in the left column may be used as "conversion factors" to change from one U.S. unit of measurement to another.

The following example shows how a conversion factor is used:

Gallons $\times$ 4 = Quarts

$\dfrac{\text{Quarts}}{4}$ = Gallons; or, Quarts $\times \frac{1}{4}$ = Gallons; also,

since $\frac{1}{4}$ = 0.25, Quarts $\times$ 0.25 = Gallons

Table 1-1 (Continued)

CAPACITY
Liquid Measure

4 fluid ounces (fl. oz.)	= 1 gill (gi.) (7.219 cu. in.)
4 gills	= 1 pint (pt.) (28.875 cu. in.)
2 pints	= 1 quart (qt.) (57.75 cu. in.)
4 quarts	= 1 gallon (gal.) (231 cu. in., or 0.134 cu. ft.)

AVOIRDUPOIS WEIGHT
(commonly used in stores, at home, etc.)

$27\frac{11}{32}$ grains (gr.)	= 1 dram (dr.)
16 drams	= 1 ounce (oz.)
16 ounces	= 1 pound (lb.) (= 7,000 gr.)
100 pounds	= 1 hundredweight (cwt.)
2,000 pounds	= 1 ton

1-2. Changing from One U.S. Unit to Another

A. To change a given unit to a smaller one:

MULTIPLY the given unit by the proper conversion factor (or factors) from Table 1-1. There will be *more* units in the smaller size.

Formula: Given Unit × Conversion Factor(s) = Smaller Unit

Example (1): Change 5 yards to feet. (length)
Solution: Given unit is yards; conversion factor, yards to feet (smaller unit), is 3:

5 yd. × 3 = 15 ft., answer

Example (2): How many pints in 6 gallons? (capacity)
Solution: Given unit is gallons; conversion factor, gallons to quarts, is 4, and quarts to pints is 2:

6 gal. × 4 × 2 = 48 pt., answer

Other examples of changing to smaller units:
Miles × 5,280 = Feet
Square Feet × 144 = Square Inches
Cubic Yards × 27 = Cubic Feet
Pounds × 16 = Ounces

B. To change a given unit to a larger one:

DIVIDE the given unit by the proper conversion factor (or factors) from Table 1-1. There will be *fewer* units in the larger size.

Formula: Given Unit ÷ Conversion Factor(s) = Larger Unit

Example (1): Change 15 feet to yards. (length)
Solution: Given unit is feet; conversion factor, feet to yards (larger unit), is 3:

15 ft. ÷ 3 = 5 yd., answer

Example (2): How many square yards in 2,592 square inches? (area)
Solution: Given unit is square inches; conversion factor, square inches to square feet, is 144, and square feet to square yards is 9:

```
        18 sq. ft.
144)2592 sq. in.
    144
    1152
    1152          18 sq. ft. ÷ 9 = 2 sq. yd., answer
```

Other examples of changing to larger units:

Feet ÷ 5,280 = Miles; or, Feet × 1/5280 = Miles
Acres ÷ 640 = Square Miles; or, Acres × 1/640
           = Square Miles
Cubic Feet ÷ 27 = Cubic Yards; or, Cubic Feet
           × 1/27 = Cubic Yards
Ounces ÷ 16 = Pounds; or, Ounces × 1/16
           = Pounds

II. THE METRIC SYSTEM OF WEIGHTS AND MEASURES

2-1. Organization of the Metric System

The metric system is a decimal system of measurement used throughout the world. The basic units of the system in everyday use are the *meter* for length, the *liter* for volume or capacity, and the *gram* for weight. For some history of the origin of the metric system, see Introduction (Sec. 3).

In the United States, Congress long ago determined that U.S. units of measurement were to be based upon standard metric units. The yard is "officially" defined as 0.9144 meter, and the pound as 0.45359237 kilogram. Other U.S. units of weights and measures are derived from these fundamental units.

In approximate terms, the meter is a little longer than a yard (about 1.1 yd.), the liter is a little more than a quart (about 1.06 qt.), and the kilogram (1,000 grams) is a little over 2 pounds (about 2.2 lb.).

Smaller and larger metric units are derived from the basic units and are designated by prefixes as follows:

micro: one millionth (0.000 001, or 1/1,000,000)
milli: one thousandth (0.001, or 1/1000)
centi: one hundredth (0.01, or 1/100)

TABLE 2-1: METRIC SYSTEM OF WEIGHTS AND MEASURES

LENGTH
(linear measure)

10 millimeters (mm.; 1 mm. = 0.001 m.)	= 1 centimeter (cm.; = 0.01 m.)
10 centimeters	= 1 decimeter (dm.; = 0.1 m.)
10 decimeters	= 1 meter (m.; = 1,000 mm.)
10 meters	= 1 dekameter (dam.)
10 dekameters	= 1 hectometer (hm.; = 100 m.)
10 hectometers	= 1 kilometer (km.; = 1,000 m.)

AREA
(square measure)

100 square millimeters (mm.^{2})	= 1 square centimeter (cm.^{2})
100 square centimeters	= 1 square decimeter (dm.^{2})
100 square decimeters	= 1 square meter (m.^{2})
100 square meters	= 1 square dekameter (dam.^{2}) or 1 are (a.)
100 square dekameters	= 1 square hectometer (hm.^{2}) or 1 hectare (ha.) (= 10,000 m.^{2})
100 square hectometers (or 100 hectares)	= 1 square kilometer (km.^{2}) (= 1,000,000 m.^{2})

VOLUME
(cubic measure)

1,000 cubic millimeters (mm.^{3})	= 1 cubic centimeter (cm.^{3}, or cc; = 0.001 l.)
1,000 cubic centimeters	= 1 cubic decimeter (dm.^{3}; = 1 l.)

(Continued on page 20)

deci: one tenth (0.1, or 1/10)
deka: ten (10)
hecto: one hundred (100)
kilo: one thousand (1,000)
mega: one million (1,000,000)

Examples: A millimeter is 1/1000 of a meter, a centimeter is 1/100 of a meter, and a kilometer is 1,000 meters. A milligram is 1/1000 of a gram, a centigram is 1/100 of a gram, and a kilogram is 1,000 grams.

Table 2-1 shows the metric system of weights and measures with "Micro" (one millionth) and "Mega" (one million) omitted for simplification.

2-2. The Decimal Nature of the Metric System

The metric system is called a "decimal" system because it is based on the number 10. You can change from one unit to another simply by multiplying or dividing by 10, 100, 1,000, or other "power" of 10.

As may be seen from Table 2-1, each metric unit of length, capacity, and weight is 10 times as large as the next smaller unit. Each unit of area is 100 (10^2) times as large as the next smaller one, and each unit of volume (cubic content) is 1,000 (10^3) times the next smaller unit.

Why metric units of area differ by 100 times:

Since 1 centimeter = 10 millimeters, when these units are "squared" to obtain area, we get 1 square centimeter = 1 cm. × 1 cm. = 10 mm. × 10 mm. = 100 mm.^{2}, or 1 square centimeter = 100 square millimeters.

19

Table 2-1 (Continued)

VOLUME

1,000 cubic decimeters	= 1 cubic meter (m.³;
	= 1,000 l.)
1,000 cubic meters	= 1 cubic dekameter (dam.³)
1,000 cubic dekameters	= 1 cubic hectometer (hm.³)
1,000 cubic hectometers	= 1 cubic kilometer (km.³)

CAPACITY

10 milliliters (ml.;	= 1 centiliter (cl.; = 0.01 l.)
1 ml. = 0.001 l.)	
10 centiliters	= 1 deciliter (dl.; = 0.1 l.)
10 deciliters	= 1 liter (l.; = 1,000 ml.)
10 liters	= 1 dekaliter (dal.)
10 dekaliters	= 1 hectoliter (hl.; = 100 l.)
10 hectoliters	= 1 kiloliter (kl.; = 1,000 l.)

WEIGHT

10 milligrams (mg.;	= 1 centigram (cg.; = 0.01 g.)
1 mg. = 0.001 g.)	
10 centigrams	= 1 decigram (dg.; = 0.1 g.)
10 decigrams	= 1 gram (g.; = 1,000 mg.)
10 grams	= 1 dekagram (dag.)
10 dekagrams	= 1 hectogram (hg.; = 100 g.)
10 hectograms	= 1 kilogram (kg.; = 1,000 g.)
1,000 kilograms	= 1 metric ton

VOLUME-CAPACITY-WEIGHT

1 cubic centimeter of water weighs	1 gram
1 milliliter of water weighs	1 gram
1 cubic decimeter of water weighs	1 kilogram
1 liter of water weighs	1 kilogram

This applies to other units of area, too. Each unit is 100 times as large as the next smaller one.

This is the same process used in developing U.S. units of area (square measure). For example, 1 foot = 12 inches; 1 square foot = 1 ft. × 1 ft. = 12 in. × 12 in. = 144 sq. in., or 1 square foot = 144 square inches.

Why metric units of volume differ by 1,000 times:

Again, since 1 centimeter = 10 millimeters, when these units are "cubed" to obtain volume or cubic content, we have 1 cubic centimeter = 1 cm. × 1 cm. × 1 cm. = 10 mm. × 10 mm. × 10 mm. = 1,000 mm.^{3}, or 1 cubic centimeter = 1,000 cubic millimeters. Other units of volume are 1,000 times as large as the next smaller unit for the same reason.

And again, this is the same process used in developing U.S. units of volume or cubic measure. For example, 1 cubic foot = 1 ft. × 1 ft. × 1 ft. = 12 in. × 12 in. × 12 in. = 1,728 cu. in., or 1 cubic foot = 1,728 cubic inches.

More about the structure and decimal nature of the metric system may be seen in Table 2-6 (page 26).

2-3. Changing from One Metric Unit to Another

The following example shows how a conversion factor from Table 2-1 is used:

Kilograms × 1,000 = Grams

$\dfrac{\text{Grams}}{1000}$ = Kilograms; or, Grams $\times \dfrac{1}{1000}$ = Kilo-

grams; or, Grams × 0.001 = Kilograms

A. To change a given unit to a smaller one:

MULTIPLY the given unit by the proper conversion factor (or factors) from Table 2-1. There will be *more* units in the smaller size.

Formula: Given Unit × Conversion Factor(s) = Smaller Unit

Example (1): Change 2 centimeters to millimeters. (length)

Solution: Given unit is centimeters; conversion factor, centimeters to millimeters (smaller unit), is 10:

2 cm. × 10 = 20 mm., answer

Example (2): How many centiliters in 3 liters? (capacity)

Solution: Given unit is liters; conversion factor, liters to deciliters is 10, and deciliters to centiliters is 10:

3 l. × 10 × 10 = 300 cl., answer

Example (3): Change 7.36 meters to smaller units.

Solutions: 7.36 m. × 10 = 73.6 decimeters
7.36 m. × 100 = 736 centimeters
7.36 m. × 1,000 = 7,360 millimeters

These are, of course, the same length expressed in different units.

An amount like 7.36 meters may also be expressed as 7 meters 36 centimeters, or 7 meters 360 millimeters.

B. To change a given unit to a larger one:

DIVIDE the given unit by the proper conversion factor (or factors) from Table 2-1. There will be *fewer* units in the larger size.

Formula: Given Unit ÷ Conversion Factor(s) = Larger Unit

Example (1): Change 4 square centimeters to square decimeters. (area)

Solution: Given unit is square centimeters; conversion factor, square centimeters to square decimeters (larger unit), is 100:

$$4 \text{ cm.}^2 \div 100 = 0.04 \text{ dm.}^2, \text{ answer}$$
or:
$$4 \text{ cm.}^2 \times 0.01 = 0.04 \text{ dm.}^2, \text{ again}$$

Example (2): How many kilometers in 440 meters? (length)

Solution: Given unit is meters; conversion factor, meters to kilometers, is 1,000 (a kilometer is 1,000 meters, and a meter is 1/1000 kilometer):

$$440 \text{ m.} \div 1,000 = 0.44 \text{ km.}, \text{ answer}$$
or:
$$440 \text{ m.} \times 0.001 = 0.44 \text{ km.}, \text{ again}$$

Example (3): Change 1,524 milligrams to larger units.
Solutions:

$$1,524 \text{ mg.} \div 10 = 152.4 \text{ centigrams (or, } 1,524 \text{ mg.}$$
$$\times 0.1 = 152.4 \text{ cg.)}$$
$$1,524 \text{ mg.} \div 100 = 15.24 \text{ decigrams (or, } 1,524 \text{ mg.}$$
$$\times 0.01 = 15.24 \text{ dg.)}$$

1,524 mg. ÷ 1,000 = 1.524 grams (or, 1,524 mg.
                         × 0.001 = 1.524 g.)

These are, of course, the same weight expressed in different units.

An amount like 1,524 milligrams may also be expressed as 152 centigrams 4 milligrams.

2-4. Multiplying by 10, 100, 1,000, etc., to Change a Metric Unit to a Smaller One

A. If the number to be multiplied has a decimal point:
Move the decimal point one place to the right for each zero in the multiplier.

Examples: Changing meters to decimeters:

3.72 m. × 10 = 37.2 dm.

Changing meters to centimeters:

3.72 m. × 100 = 372 cm.

Changing meters to millimeters:

3.72 m. × 1,000 = 3,720 mm. (a zero attached to provide the extra place needed)

B. If the number to be multiplied has no decimal point:
Attach one zero to the number for each zero in the multiplier.

Examples: Changing liters to deciliters:

12 l. × 10 = 120 dl.

Changing liters to centiliters:

12 l. × 100 = 1,200 cl.

Changing liters to milliliters:

12 l. × 1,000 = 12,000 ml.

2-5. Dividing by 10, 100, 1,000, etc., to Change a Metric Unit to a Larger One

To divide a number by 10, move the decimal point one place to the left; to divide by 100, move the decimal point two places to the left; to divide by 1,000, move the decimal point three places to the left, etc. The decimal point is moved one place to the left for each zero in the divisor.

Keep in mind that dividing by 10 is the same as multiplying by 1/10 or by 0.1; dividing by 100 is the same as multiplying by 1/100 or by 0.01; dividing by 1,000 is the same as multiplying by 1/1000 or by 0.001, and so on.

Examples: Changing milligrams to centigrams:
486 mg. ÷ 10 = 48.6 cg. (or, 486 mg. × 0.1
= 48.6 cg.)

Changing milligrams to decigrams:
486 mg. ÷ 100 = 4.86 dg. (or, 486 mg. × 0.01
= 4.86 dg.)

Changing milligrams to grams:
486 mg. ÷ 1,000 = 0.486 g. (or, 486 mg. × 0.001
= 0.486 g.)

TABLE 2-6: INTERRELATION OF PREFIXES FOR METRIC UNITS OF LENGTH, CAPACITY, AND WEIGHT

"No Prefix" refers to base unit: Meter, Liter, or Gram

Given → Multiply to find	Milli	Centi	Deci	No Prefix	Deka	Hecto	Kilo
Milli	1	0.1	0.01	0.001	0.0001	0.000 01	0.000 001
Centi	10	1	0.1	0.01	0.001	0.0001	0.000 01
Deci	100	10	1	0.1	0.01	0.001	0.0001
No Prefix }	1,000	100	10	1	0.1	0.01	0.001
Deka	10,000	1,000	100	10	1	0.1	0.01
Hecto	100,000	10,000	1,000	100	10	1	0.1
Kilo	1,000,000	100,000	10,000	1,000	100	10	1

2-6. Ready-Reference Table for Changing Metric Units from One to Another

Table 2-6 shows the interrelation of prefixes for the metric units of length, capacity, and weight. "No Prefix" refers to the base unit without a prefix—meter(s), liter(s), or gram(s). The table may be used as follows to change from one unit to another.

Find the given prefix (No Prefix indicates a unit without a prefix) in the column on the left, follow this row to the right to the column under the prefix desired, and multiply by the factor shown.

Example (1): Change 140 centimeters to meters.
Solution: Given prefix is "Centi"; desired unit is "meters" (No Prefix). Find Centi in the left column and follow this row to the column for No Prefix. The conversion factor is 0.01:

140 cm. $\times$ 0.01 = 1.4 meters, answer

Example (2): Change 2 kilograms to centigrams.
Solution: Find Kilo in the left column and follow this row to the Centi column; conversion factor is 100,000:

2 kg. $\times$ 100,000 = 200,000 centigrams, answer

Table 2-6 may also be applied to changing metric units of area and volume.

To change from one metric unit of AREA to another:

Find the conversion factor as before and multiply by this factor twice.

Example: Change 3 square centimeters to square millimeters.

Solution: Prefix given is Centi; conversion factor for changing to"Milli" is 10. Multiply by 10 twice:

3 cm.² × 10 × 10 = 300 square millimeters, answer

To change from one metric unit of VOLUME to another:

Find the conversion factor as before and multiply by this factor three times.

Example: Change 2 cubic meters to cubic centimeters.

Solution: Given unit, meters, has No Prefix; conversion factor for changing to Centi is 100. Multiply by 100 three times:

2 m.³ × 100 × 100 × 100 = 2,000,000 cubic
centimeters, answer

2-7. Another Easy Way to Change from One Metric Unit to Another

Arrange the prefixes as shown below. Again, No Prefix refers to the base unit without a prefix: meter(s), liter(s), or gram(s).

No
Kilo Hecto Deka Prefix Deci Centi Milli

To change from one unit to another, start with the prefix *given* and count the number of places to the prefix *desired.*

If you count to the RIGHT, move the decimal point in the given unit that many places to the RIGHT (or add that many zeros.) If you count to the LEFT, move the decimal point that many places to the LEFT.

Example (1): Change 12 kilometers to meters.
Solution: Start with Kilo (given) and count the 3 places to the right to No Prefix (meters); add 3 zeros to kilometers:

12 kilometers = 12,000 meters, answer

Example (2): Change 1.35 grams to centigrams.
Solution: Count 2 places to the right from No Prefix (grams, given) to Centi; move the decimal point 2 places to the right:

1.35 grams = 135 centigrams, answer

Example (3): Change 125 milliliters to centiliters.
Solution: Count 1 place to the left from Milli to Centi; move the decimal point 1 place to the left:

125 milliliters = 12.5 centiliters, answer

To change from one unit of AREA to another:

Double the number of places counted and proceed as before.

Example: Change 314 square millimeters to square centimeters.
Solution: Count 1 place to the left from Milli to Centi; double this to 2 places; move the decimal point 2 places to the left:

314 square millimeters = 3.14 square centimeters,
answer

To change from one unit of VOLUME to another:

Triple the number of places counted and proceed as before.

Example: Change 3 cubic meters to cubic centimeters.
Solution: Count 2 places to the right from No Prefix (meters) to Centi; triple this to 6 places; add 6 zeros to cubic meters:

3 cubic meters = 3,000,000 cubic centimeters,
answer

2-8. Metric Units Most Commonly Used in Everyday Life

Just as little use is made of drams, furlongs, fathoms, or pecks in U.S. units, some metric units are not ordinarily used in daily life.

The most commonly used metric units are the meter, liter, and gram, and units with the prefixes milli (1/1000), centi (1/100), and kilo (1,000). Units with the prefixes deci (1/10), deka (10), or hecto (100) are infrequently, or even rarely, used.

The metric units of weights and measures commonly used in everyday life are arranged in Table 2-8 for easy reference.

NOTE: Periods are not used with symbols in the International Metric System (SI), but *are* used in this book as an aid to beginners accustomed to periods after abbreviations of U.S. units. Many will feel more "at home" with this style when first changing to metric. Furthermore, in the case of "1." for liter, the period serves to distinguish the symbol from "1," the numeral, and thus helps to avoid confusion. The book also does not follow SI in the spelling of "metre" and "litre," or in the use of a space (10 000) instead of a comma (10,000) in numbers of four or more digits.

TABLE 2-8: METRIC UNITS COMMONLY USED IN EVERYDAY LIFE

LENGTH

1 centimeter	=	10 millimeters
1 meter	=	100 centimeters
1 meter	=	1,000 millimeters
1 kilometer	=	1,000 meters

km. $\times$ 1,000 = m. $\times$ 100 = cm. $\times$ 10 = mm.
mm. $\times$ 0.1 = cm. $\times$ 0.01 = m. $\times$ 0.001 = km.

AREA

1 square centimeter	=	100 square millimeters
1 square meter	=	10,000 square centimeters

m.^{2} $\times$ 10,000 = cm.^{2} $\times$ 100 = mm.^{2}
mm.^{2} $\times$ 0.01 = cm.^{2} $\times$ 0.0001 = m.^{2}

VOLUME

1 cubic centimeter	=	1,000 cubic millimeters
1 cubic meter	=	1,000,000 cubic centimeters

m.^{3} $\times$ 1,000,000 = cm.^{3} $\times$ 1,000 = mm.^{3}
mm.^{3} $\times$ 0.001 = cm.^{3} $\times$ 0.000 001 = m.^{3}

CAPACITY

1 centiliter	=	10 milliliters
1 liter	=	1,000 milliliters
1 liter	=	100 centiliters

l. $\times$ 100 = cl. $\times$ 10 = ml.
ml. $\times$ 0.1 = cl. $\times$ 0.01 = l.

WEIGHT

1 gram	=	1,000 milligrams
1 kilogram	=	1,000 grams
1 metric ton	=	1,000 kilograms

metric ton $\times$ 1,000 = kg. $\times$ 1,000 = g. $\times$ 1,000 = mg.
mg. $\times$ 0.001 = g. $\times$ 0.001 = kg. $\times$ 0.001 = metric ton

III. GOING FROM THE U.S. TO THE METRIC SYSTEM

3-1. Measurements and Calculations

It's about as easy to measure with a ruler marked in centimeters as with one marked in inches, or to read a scale in kilograms as in pounds, or to buy milk by the liter as by the quart. Metric and customary measuring devices are about equally easy to use. It's simply a matter of getting used to the way a device is calibrated.

But when it comes to *calculations* with measurements, metric is generally easier to work with. For example, it's easier to change metric units from one to another than to change U.S. units from one to another because metric is a decimal system and the U.S. system is not.

For instance, to change a metric length of 112 centimeters to larger units, you need only move the decimal point to the left. Thus: 112 centimeters = 11.2 decimeters = 1.12 meters. But to change 112 inches to feet and to yards, you have to divide by 12 and by 3, and work your way through fractions and "mixed numbers":

$$112 \text{ inches} \div 12 = 9\frac{4}{12} = 9\frac{1}{3} \text{ feet}; \div 3 = 3\frac{1}{9} \text{ yards. Or,}$$

if you prefer, 3 yards 4 inches.

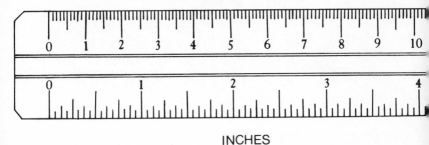

CENTIMETERS

INCHES

Changing other U.S. units can be even more difficult. Consider these exercises in multiplication and long division: To change cubic feet to cubic inches, multiply cubic feet by 1,728; gallons to fluid ounces, multiply gallons by 128; feet to miles, divide feet by 5,280; square inches to square feet, divide square inches by 144. And then, of course, there are three kinds of ounces: fluid, troy, and avoirdupois; and two kinds of pints and quarts: liquid and dry; and two lengths of miles: land and nautical; and a ton can be either "long" or "short"!

In the metric system, on the other hand, changing units is easier since any metric unit may be changed to a larger one by simply moving the decimal point to the left, or to a smaller one by moving the decimal point to the right.

Now, what about the *addition* of measurements in U.S. units and in metric units? Judge for yourself which is easier in the following example:

U.S.	Metric
7 ft. 4 in.	2,200 mm.
3 ft. 9 in.	1,125 mm.
9 ft. 5 in.	2,825 mm.
19 ft. 18 in. = 20 ft. 6 in.	6,150 mm. = 6.15 m.
= 6 yd. 2 ft. 6 in.	

By using the conversion factors shown in Table 3-3, you will see that 6 yd. 2 ft. 6 in. = 6.15 m.

Next, let's consider an example in square measure. If a room measures 14 feet 4 inches long and 9 feet 6 inches wide, what is its area in square yards? (9 sq. ft. = 1 sq. yd.)

Solution: Length × Width = Area

(a) 14 ft. 4 in. = $14\frac{1}{3} = \frac{43}{3}$ ft.; 9 ft. 6 in. = $9\frac{1}{2} = \frac{19}{2}$ ft.

(b) $\frac{43}{3}$ ft. × $\frac{19}{2}$ ft. = $\frac{817}{6}$ sq. ft.

computation:
$$\begin{array}{r} 43 \\ \times\ 19 \\ \hline 387 \\ 43 \\ \hline 817 \end{array}$$

(c) $\frac{817}{6}$ sq. ft. × $\frac{1}{9} = \frac{817}{54} = 15\frac{7}{54}$ sq. yd., answer computation:

$$\begin{array}{r} 15 \\ 54\overline{)817} \\ \underline{54} \\ 277 \\ \underline{270} \\ 7 \end{array}$$

The same room measured in metric units would be 4.3 meters long and 2.85 meters wide. See how much easier it is to find its area:

$$\begin{array}{r} 2.85 \text{ m.} \\ \times\ \ 4.3 \text{ m.} \\ \hline 855 \\ 1140\ \ \ \\ \hline 12.255 \text{ square meters} \end{array}$$

Here's another example of how metric can save time in working with square measure. How many acres are there in 79,866 square yards? To find out, you can divide square yards by $30\frac{1}{4}$ to obtain square rods, and divide square rods by 160 to get acres. Or since there are 4,840 square yards to the acre ($30\frac{1}{4} \times 160 = 4,840$), you can do it in one step:

$$\begin{array}{r} 16 \\ 4840\overline{)79866} \\ \underline{4840}\ \ \ \\ 31466 \\ \underline{29040}\ \\ 2426 \end{array}$$

$$16\frac{2426}{4840} = 16\frac{1213}{2420} \text{ acres, answer (about } 16\frac{1}{2} \text{ acres)}$$

But if we have 79,866 square *meters* and want to find out how many hectares there are, the calculation is much easier: 79,866 m.² ÷ 10,000 = 7.9866 (about 8) hectares.

And changing hectares to square meters is just as easy: 7.9866 hectares × 10,000 = 79,866 square meters, whereas changing acres to square yards requires multiplying acres by 4,840.

And finally, let's try an example in cubic measure. If a box holds 2 cubic yards, how many cubic inches would it contain? (1 cu. yd. = 27 cu. ft.; 1 cu. ft. = 1,728 cu. in.)

2 cu. yd. × 27 = 54 cu. ft.

$$\begin{array}{r} 1728 \\ \times\ \ 54 \\ \hline 6912 \\ 8640 \\ \hline 93312 \end{array}$$ cubic inches, answer

But if a box holds 2 cubic *meters*, its volume in cubic centimeters is easily found this way: 2 m.³ × 1,000 = 2,000; × 1,000 = 2,000,000 cubic centimeters. Or, 2 × 1,000,000 = 2,000,000, again.

3-2. Thinking Metric and Converting to Metric

In learning to use metric, there is a place for both *thinking metric* and *converting to metric*, as may be seen in the following example.

If you have a metric tape measure and want to

measure a fence in meters, you simply apply the tape in the usual way. Let's say that you find the fence to be 6.3 meters long. By using a metric measuring device and thinking in metric terms, you obtained the length directly in metric units. There was no need to convert.

But suppose the only tape you have is one calibrated in feet and inches. To find the fence's length in meters, you would measure in U.S. units and *convert* to metric. After finding that the fence measures 21 feet, you multiply this by the conversion factor 0.3 (Table 3–3): 21 ft. × 0.3 = 6.3 meters, again. It's the same length no matter how you measure it, and whether you express it in feet or meters.

As you can see, to get a metric "answer," it's easier to measure in metric units—provided you have the necessary metric measuring device. But if you don't, you'll have to convert, and a conversion table will be a handy little helper to have around.

A. Learning to think and use metric:

Since metric is a measuring "language," it's better to be able to "think" in this language and not think in the old units and "translate" to the new. However, for anyone accustomed to using only the customary units, learning to think metric will require application and practice.

Only a small part of the metric system need be learned for everyday uses. Who knows and uses all the U.S. units: fathoms, rods, grains, pecks, chains, and so on? Probably no one. We are most familiar with whatever units we use in daily life: inches, feet, pounds, etc. It's the same with metric. Only the most commonly used units need be learned for everyday use (see Table 2–8, page 31).

If measuring acres is not part of your life, you will have just as little need for hectares, so you can omit this unit from your basic metric vocabulary. You might do the same with dekameters, cubic meters, metric tons, or any other units not of immediate interest. Motivate yourself by learning only what you need and can put to practical use. Don't try to learn metric in the "abstract"—as an exercise or a drill. This will rob metric of its *meaning*.

Once you have decided what metric units *you* will need to use, think of these in relation to familiar objects. A Lincoln penny, for example, is about 19 millimeters wide, a dime about 18; 2 paper clips weigh about a gram, a nickel about 5 grams, a large egg a little over 55 grams, a medium-size tomato about 140 grams. With food packages being marked in both customary and metric units, use these to help visualize capacity in milliliters and liters, and weight in grams and kilograms.

To think temperature in Celsius degrees, remember that water freezes at 0° and boils at 100°, normal body temperature is 37°, and a room will feel comfortable at around 20° to 22°.

In a car, when the speedometer reads 40 (mi. per hr.), think of your metric speed as "64" (km. per hr.); at 50, think of your speed as "80"; at 60, think of it as "96." This is really "converting" rather than "thinking metric" but it's about the best you can do without a speedometer that reads in metric.

Another aid to thinking metric is to measure familiar objects in metric units. To measure short lengths, all you need is a 30-centimeter ruler or a meter stick. Measure, for example, the height of a table, the width of a door, the length of a finger. With a metric tape measure, you can measure your height and your waistline. This practice in metric measurement will give you the "feel" of the metric units and some objects to remember in reference to these units.

For measuring areas and volumes in metric units, see Sections 4-3 and 4-4. For measuring capacity, use a metric measuring cup or a liter measure; and for weighing in metric, you will need a metric scale—something you are not likely to find in the average home (more on metric measurements in Chapter IX).

B. Converting from U.S. to metric:

When a measurement is made or given in U.S. units and you want it in metric (or the other way around), the units must be "translated" from one measuring language to the other. This can be done by using the conversion tables in this book.

A conversion table is like a two-language dictionary. Starting with a word in one language, you can consult the dictionary to find the equivalent word in the other language. Likewise, when you have an amount expressed in a unit of one measurement system, you can find its equivalent in the other system by using a conversion table.

"Going metric" doesn't mean throwing away our 10-quart pails, or the bathroom scale that reads in pounds. Grandma isn't likely to part with the 5-foot measuring tape she uses for sewing, nor is Dad apt to trade in the family car because its speedometer reads in miles instead of kilometers. And Mom will probably keep using the kitchen stove until it wears out even though its oven temperature is controlled in Fahrenheit degrees and not in Celsius.

Countless other products are also calibrated in customary units: pots and pans, electric blenders, coffee makers, thermometers, tools, meters, appliances, measuring devices, etc. Until these wear out or are thrown out and replaced by metric products, the customary units will need to be converted to metric units. Customary measurements given in textbooks, cookbooks, instruction books, etc., will need conversion, too, until new books in metric measure replace the old.

In making a conversion, be guided by the rule of common sense. Determine first how exact the conversion must be to suit your purpose. In converting from inches to millimeters, for example, "about" 25 millimeters per inch will be close enough for most everyday purposes, but 25.4 per inch will be necessary for precision work, as in a laboratory or a machine shop (1 inch = "exactly" 25.4 millimeters).

Keep things simple by using a conversion factor with as few places as practicable. For instance, a pound is equal to 0.4536 kilogram (to four decimal places) but using this to convert a pound of potatoes would be silly. Better to "round off" 0.4536 to a less frightening figure like 0.5 and say that a pound of potatoes weighs about a half kilogram (0.5 kg.), which is close enough for all practical purposes. Round off conversion factors like this whenever you can. It's especially useful for making fast estimates or mental conversions (more on this in Section 9-4).

The examples in this book are not just "exercises" in converting from one measuring system to another. Instead, they show *practical applications* of the metric units you are likely to meet in everyday life. The conversion tables are designed for practical use, too. They are in simplified form and include only the most commonly used units. Use these tables for making conversions when necessary but keep in mind that the more you think metric, the less you need to convert.

3-3. Approximate Equivalents of U.S. and Metric Units for Everyday Use

The conversion factors in Table 3–3 are approximate (not "exact") but are close enough for most everyday needs in converting from U.S. to metric units, or from metric to U.S. (The table is on the next 2 pages.)

To use Table 3-3, find the known or given unit in the left column and multiply by the conversion factor for the desired unit in the right column.

Example (1): How many meters in 20 feet?

Solution: Under LENGTH, find the line with "Feet" in the left column and "Meters" on the right; conversion factor is 0.3:

$$20 \text{ ft.} \times 0.3 = 6 \text{ m., answer}$$

Example (2): Convert 30 liters to quarts.

Solution: Under CAPACITY (liquid measure), find the line with "Liters" on the left and "Quarts" on the right; conversion factor is 1.06:

$$30 \text{ l.} \times 1.06 = 31.8 \text{ qt., answer}$$

TABLE 3-3: APPROXIMATE CONVERSION FACTORS: U.S. AND METRIC UNITS

LENGTH

Inches	× 25	= Millimeters
Inches	× 2.5	= Centimeters
Feet	× 30	= Centimeters
Feet	× 0.3	= Meters
Yards	× 90	= Centimeters
Yards	× 0.9	= Meters
Rods	× 5	= Meters
Miles	× 1.6	= Kilometers
Millimeters	× 0.04	= Inches
Centimeters	× 0.4	= Inches
Centimeters	× 0.033	= Feet
Meters	× 40	= Inches
Meters	× 3.3	= Feet
Meters	× 1.1	= Yards
Meters	× 0.2	= Rods
Kilometers	× 0.62	= Miles

AREA

Square Inches	× 6.5	= Square Centimeters
Square Feet	× 0.09	= Square Meters
Square Yards	× 0.84	= Square Meters
Acres	× 0.4	= Hectares
Square Miles	× 2.6	= Square Kilometers
Square Centimeters	× 0.16	= Square Inches
Square Meters	× 11	= Square Feet
Square Meters	× 1.2	= Square Yards
Hectares	× 2.5	= Acres
Square Kilometers	× 0.4	= Square Miles

VOLUME

Cubic Inches	× 16.4	= Cubic Centimeters
Cubic Feet	× 0.03	= Cubic Meters
Cubic Yards	× 0.76	= Cubic Meters
Cubic Centimeters	× 0.06	= Cubic Inches
Cubic Meters	× 35	= Cubic Feet
Cubic Meters	× 1.3	= Cubic Yards

CAPACITY
Dry Measure

Bushels	× 35	= Liters
Liters	× 0.03	= Bushels

Liquid Measure

Fluid Ounces	× 30	= Milliliters
Pints	× 473	= Milliliters
Pints	× 0.47	= Liters
Quarts	× 0.95	= Liters
Gallons	× 3.8	= Liters
Milliliters	× 0.034	= Fluid Ounces
Milliliters	× 0.002	= Pints
Liters	× 2.1	= Pints
Liters	× 1.06	= Quarts
Liters	× 0.26	= Gallons

WEIGHT

Ounces	× 28	= Grams
Ounces	× 0.028	= Kilograms
Pounds	× 454	= Grams
Pounds	× 0.45	= Kilograms
Tons	× 0.9	= Metric Tons
Grams	× 0.035	= Ounces
Grams	× 0.002	= Pounds
Kilograms	× 35	= Ounces
Kilograms	× 2.2	= Pounds
Metric Tons	× 1.1	= Tons

The conversion factors in Table 3–3, and the equivalents in Table 3–4 that follows, show the relationships between pairs of common U.S. and metric units. You might memorize any of these for which you find frequent use as you learn to think metric.

3-4. U.S.-Metric Equivalents in Whole Numbers

Table 3-4 shows the approximate equivalents of certain U.S. and metric units in whole numbers, with the U.S. units in quantities of 1, 10, or 100. The equivalents have been simplified by eliminating the use of common fractions and decimals.

The table shows, for example, that for every 10 feet, there are 3 meters; in every 100 cubic feet, there are 3 cubic meters; in every 100 quarts, 95 liters; and that every 100 pounds weigh in at 45 kilograms.

TABLE 3-4: APPROXIMATE EQUIVALENTS OF CERTAIN U.S. AND METRIC UNITS IN WHOLE NUMBERS

LENGTH

1 inch	=	25 millimeters
1 foot	=	30 centimeters
1 yard	=	90 centimeters
1 mile	=	1,600 meters
10 inches	=	25 centimeters
10 feet	=	3 meters
10 yards	=	9 meters
10 miles	=	16 kilometers
100 yards	=	90 meters
100 miles	=	160 kilometers

Table 3-4 (Continued)

AREA

10 square inches	=	65 square centimeters
10 acres	=	4 hectares
10 square miles	=	26 square kilometers
100 square feet	=	9 square meters
100 square yards	=	84 square meters

VOLUME

10 cubic inches	=	164 cubic centimeters
100 cubic feet	=	3 cubic meters
100 cubic yards	=	76 cubic meters

CAPACITY

1 bushel	=	35 liters
1 fluid ounce	=	30 milliliters
1 pint	=	473 milliliters
10 gallons	=	38 liters
100 quarts	=	95 liters

WEIGHT

1 ounce	=	28 grams
1 pound	=	454 grams
10 tons	=	9 metric tons
100 pounds	=	45 kilograms

IV. CONVERTING TO METRIC FOR EVERYDAY USE

The conversions in this chapter are based upon the approximate conversion factors of Table 3-3 (except as noted in Sec. 4-2). Measuring in metric will require using metric rulers, tapes, liter measures, etc.

The examples show practical applications of units as generally employed for the type of measurement involved. For example, inches and feet for short lengths are converted to millimeters and centimeters; feet and yards for longer lengths are converted to centimeters and meters; miles are given for distances and converted to kilometers. The same applies to the units used for area, volume, capacity, and weight.

4-1. Units of Length

Example (1): INCHES to MILLIMETERS: If a sheet of paper is 8 inches wide, what is its width in millimeters? (dimensions of paper will be in millimeters)

Method: Inches × 25 = Millimeters
Solution: 8 in. × 25 = 200 mm., answer

Example (2): INCHES to CENTIMETERS: If a waist measurement is 40 inches, what is it in centimeters? (clothing sizes will use centimeters)

Method: Inches × 2.5 = Centimeters
Solution: 40 in. × 2.5 = 100 cm., answer

Example (3): FEET to CENTIMETERS: If a man is 6 feet tall, what is his height in centimeters?

YARD

feet

1 2 3

centimeters

100

METER

Method: Feet × 30 = Centimeters
Solution: 6 ft. × 30 = 180 cm., answer

Example (4): FEET AND INCHES to CENTI-
METERS: If a board is 3 feet 4 inches long, what is its
length in centimeters?

Method (a): Change to inches and multiply by 2.5
(cm. per in.).
Solution:

(a) 3 ft. × 12 = 36 in.; + 4 in. = 40 in., length in
inches

(b) 40 in. × 2.5 = 100 cm., length in centimeters,
answer

Method (b): Change to feet and multiply by 30 (cm.
per ft.).
Solution:

(a) 3 ft. 4 in. = $3\frac{1}{3}$ ft. = $\frac{10}{3}$ ft., length in feet

(b) $\frac{10}{\cancel{3}}$ ft. × $\cancel{30}^{10}$ = 100 cm., again

47

Example (5): FEET to METERS: If a room is 20 feet long, how long is it in meters?
Method: Feet × 0.3 = Meters
Solution: 20 ft. × 0.3 = 6 m., answer

Example (6): YARDS to CENTIMETERS: If you need 5 yards of material, how many centimeters would this be?
Method: Yards × 90 = Centimeters
Solution: 5 yd. × 90 = 450 cm., answer

Example (7): YARDS to METERS: A football field is 100 yards long (without end zones). How many meters?
Method: Yards × 0.9 = Meters
Solution: 100 yd. × 0.9 = 90 m., answer

Example (8): MILES to KILOMETERS: If the next town is 6 miles away, what is this distance in kilometers?
Method: Miles × 1.6 = Kilometers
Solution: 6 mi. × 1.6 = 9.6 km., answer

Example (9): ADDITION OF LENGTHS: If a piece of wood is 1 meter long and another is 14 centimeters in length, what is their combined length?
Method: Change both lengths to the same unit, then add.
Solution 1: 1 m. = 100 cm.; + 14 cm. = 114 cm., answer
Solution 2: 14 cm. = 0.14 m.; + 1 m. = 1.14 m. (the same length as 114 cm. but expressed in a different unit)

Examples comparing the use of U.S. and metric units in calculations with lengths are given in Section 3-1.

For approximate equivalents of U.S. and metric distances commonly used in sports events, see Table A, page 92.

4-2. Converting Fractions of an Inch to Millimeters

The following examples use the *exact* equivalent of 1 inch = 25.4 millimeters.

Example (1): How many millimeters in $\frac{1}{4}$ inch?
Method: Fraction of Inch × 25.4 = Millimeters
Solution: $\frac{1}{4}$ in. × 25.4 = 6.35 mm., answer

Example (2): How many millimeters in 0.01 inch?
Solution: 0.01 in. × 25.4 = 0.254 mm., answer

Table B (page 93) shows common fractions of an inch by thirty-seconds and their equivalents in millimeters.

4-3. Units of Area (square measure)

Example (1): AREA MEASURED IN METRIC UNITS: If a room is 5 meters long and 3 meters wide, what is its area in square meters?
Formula: Length × Width = Area of a Rectangle
Solution: 5 m. × 3 m. = 15 square meters (m.²), answer

In multiplying units of length to obtain area, the units multiplied must be alike and the answer will be in this unit "squared."

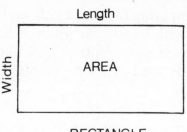

Length

Width

AREA

RECTANGLE

Examples:
Millimeters × Millimeters = *Square* Millimeters
(mm.²)

Centimeters × Centimeters = *Square* Centimeters
(cm.²)

Example (2): SQUARE INCHES to SQUARE
CENTIMETERS: If a sheet of paper measures 8 by 12
inches, what is its area in square centimeters?

Method: Find the area in square inches and multiply
by 6.5 (cm.² per sq. in.).

Solution:

(a) 8 in. × 12 in. = 96 sq. in., area in square inches

(b) 96 sq. in. × 6.5 = 624 cm.², area in square centimeters, answer

Example (3): SQUARE FEET to SQUARE
METERS: If a room is 12 feet long and 10 feet wide,
what is its area in square meters?

Method: Square Feet × 0.09 = Square Meters

Solution: 12 ft. × 10 ft. = 120 sq. ft.; × 0.09 =
10.8 m.², answer

Example (4): ACRES to HECTARES: If a farm has an area of 20 acres, what is its area in hectares?

Method: Acres × 0.4 = Hectares

Solution: 20 acres × 0.4 = 8 ha., answer

Example (5): SQUARE MILES to SQUARE KILO-METERS: If a park has an area of 9 square miles, what is its area in square kilometers?

Method: Square Miles × 2.6 = Square Kilometers

Solution: 9 sq. mi. × 2.6 = 23.4 km.², answer

Examples comparing the use of U.S. and metric units in calculations with square and cubic measurements are given in Section 3-1.

4-4. Units of Volume (cubic measure)

Example (1): VOLUME MEASURED IN METRIC UNITS: If a box is 30 centimeters long, 10 centimeters wide, and 12 centimeters high, what is its volume in cubic centimeters?

Formula: Length × Width × Height = Volume or Cubic Content (of a rectangular solid or box)

Solution: 30 cm. × 10 cm. × 12 cm. = 3,600 cm.³, answer

In multiplying units of length to obtain volume or cubic content, the units multiplied must be alike and the answer will be in this unit "cubed."

Examples:

Millimeters × Millimeters × Millimeters = *Cubic* Millimeters (mm.³)

Meters × Meters × Meters = *Cubic* Meters (m.³)

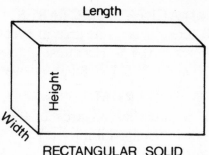

Length

Height

Width

RECTANGULAR SOLID

Example (2): CUBIC INCHES to CUBIC CENTI-METERS: If the volume of a box is 8 cubic inches, how many cubic centimeters would this be?

Method: Cubic Inches × 16.4 = Cubic Centimeters
Solution: 8 cu. in. × 16.4 = 131.2 cm.^{3}, answer

Example (3): CUBIC FEET to CUBIC METERS: If the inside of a rectangular box is 3 feet long, 2 feet wide, and 4 feet high, how many cubic meters will it hold?

Method: Cubic Feet × 0.03 = Cubic Meters
Solution:
(a) 3 ft. × 2 ft. × 4 ft. = 24 cu. ft.
(b) 24 cu. ft. × 0.03 = 0.72 m.^{3}, answer

Example (4): CUBIC YARDS to CUBIC METERS: How many cubic meters are there in 4 cubic yards of sand?

Method: Cubic Yards × 0.76 = Cubic Meters
Solution: 4 cu. yd. × 0.76 = 3.04 m.^{3}, answer

For more about computing with measurement numbers, see Section 9–3.

4-5. Units of Capacity

Example (1): BUSHELS to LITERS: If you have 2 bushels of corn, how many liters would this be?
Method: Bushels × 35 = Liters
Solution: 2 bu. × 35 = 70 l., answer

Example (2): FLUID OUNCES to MILLILITERS: If a bottle contains 2 fluid ounces of medicine, how much is this in milliliters?
Method: Fluid Ounces × 30 = Milliliters
Solution: 2 fl. oz. × 30 = 60 ml., answer

Example (3): PINTS to LITERS: How many liters in 3 pints of milk?
Method: Pints × 0.47 = Liters
Solution: 3 pt. × 0.47 = 1.41 l., answer

Example (4): QUARTS to LITERS: How many liters of water are needed to fill a 10-quart pail?
Method: Quarts × 0.95 = Liters
Solution: 10 qt. × 0.95 = 9.5 l., answer

Example (5): GALLONS to LITERS: If you buy 10 gallons of gasoline, how many liters would this be?
Method: Gallons × 3.8 = Liters
Solution: 10 gal. × 3.8 = 38 l., answer

4-6. Units of Weight

Example (1): OUNCES to GRAMS: If a bag of fruit weighs 8½ ounces, what is its weight in grams?
Method: Ounces × 28 = Grams

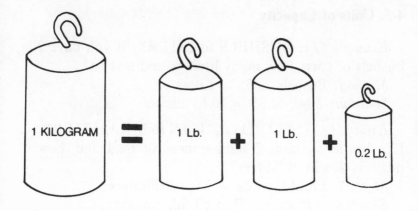

1 KILOGRAM = 1 Lb. + 1 Lb. + 0.2 Lb.

Solution: 8 oz. × 28 = 224 g.
   ½ oz. × 28 = <u>14</u> g.
                238 g., answer

Example (2): POUNDS to KILOGRAMS: If a woman weighs 120 pounds, what is her weight in kilograms?

Method: Pounds × 0.45 = Kilograms
Solution: 120 lb. × 0.45 = 54 kg., answer

Example (3): POUNDS AND OUNCES to KILOGRAMS: If a piece of meat weighs 6 pounds 5 ounces, how many kilograms ("kilos") would this be?

Solution: 6 lb. × 0.45 = 2.70 kg.
   5 oz. × 0.028 = <u>.14</u> kg.
                2.84 kg., answer

Example (4): TONS to METRIC TONS: How many metric tons in 3 U.S. tons of coal?

Method: Tons × 0.9 = Metric Tons
Solution: 3 tons × 0.9 = 2.7 metric tons, answer

4-7. Converting Unit Prices from U.S. to Metric Units

Table 4-7 shows conversion factors that may be used for approximate conversions of unit prices from U.S. to metric units, as in the following examples.

Example (1): PRICE PER SQUARE YARD to PRICE PER SQUARE METER: If a carpet sells for $12 a square yard, what is its price per square meter?
Solution: $12 per sq. yd. × 1.2 (conversion factor) = $14.40 per m.², answer

Example (2): PRICE PER POUND to PRICE PER KILOGRAM: If a cut of meat sells for $1.20 per pound, what is its unit price per kilogram?
Solution: $1.20 per lb. × 2.2 (conversion factor) = $2.64 per kg., answer

TABLE 4-7: APPROXIMATE CONVERSIONS OF UNIT PRICES FROM U.S. TO METRIC UNITS

Price per foot	× 3.3	= Price per meter
Price per yard	× 1.1	= Price per meter
Price per square foot	× 11	= Price per square meter
Price per square yard	× 1.2	= Price per square meter
Price per 100 square feet	× 0.11	= Price per square meter
Price per fluid ounce	× 0.034	= Price per milliliter
Price per pint	× 2.1	= Price per liter
Price per quart	× 1.06	= Price per liter
Price per gallon	× 0.26	= Price per liter
Price per ounce	× 0.035	= Price per gram
Price per pound	× 2.2	= Price per kilogram

The conversion factors of Table 4-7 may also be used to convert $1 of cost or price per U.S. unit to $1 per metric unit.

Examples:

$1 per pound	× 2.2	= $2.20 per kilogram
$1 per foot	× 3.3	= $3.30 per meter
$1 per yard	× 1.1	= $1.10 per meter
$1 per square foot	× 11	= $11 per square meter
$1 per square yard	× 1.2	= $1.20 per square meter
$1 per quart	× 1.06	= $1.06 per liter
$1 per gallon	× 0.26	= $0.26 per liter

To find the unit price in *any* unit, U.S. or metric, divide the price of the package by the number of units in the package.

Formula: $\dfrac{\text{Price of Package}}{\text{Number of Units}} = $ Price Per Unit (unit price)

Example (1): If a box of cookies weighs 7 ounces and sells for $.35, what is its price per pound?

Solution: $\dfrac{\$.35 \text{ price}}{7 \text{ oz.}} = \$.05$ per oz.; × 16 (oz. per lb.)
$= \$.80$ per lb., answer

Example (2): If a carpet has an area of 20 square meters and sells for $280, what is its price per square meter?

Solution: $\dfrac{\overset{14}{\cancel{\$280}} \text{ price}}{\underset{}{\cancel{20} \text{ m.}^2}} = \$14$ per m.^{2}, answer

V. CONVERSIONS BETWEEN FAHRENHEIT AND CELSIUS (CENTIGRADE) TEMPERATURES

5-1. Fahrenheit and Celsius Scales

The Fahrenheit (F.) scale, long used in the United States for everyday temperature measurement, is being replaced by the Celsius (C.) scale of the metric system. The Celsius scale (formerly called centigrade) is used for scientific work throughout the world.

The relationship between the Fahrenheit and Celsius scales may be seen in Figure 5-1. Some thermometers have both scales so that the temperature can be read either way. To measure temperatures in metric, use a Celsius scale.

5-2. Converting Fahrenheit and Celsius (Centigrade) Temperatures from One to the Other

A. To convert Fahrenheit to Celsius:

Subtract 32 from the Fahrenheit degrees and multiply by 5/9.

Formula: $(\text{F. Degrees} - 32) \times \dfrac{5}{9} = \text{C. Degrees}$

$$\frac{5}{9}(\text{F.} - 32) = \text{C.}$$

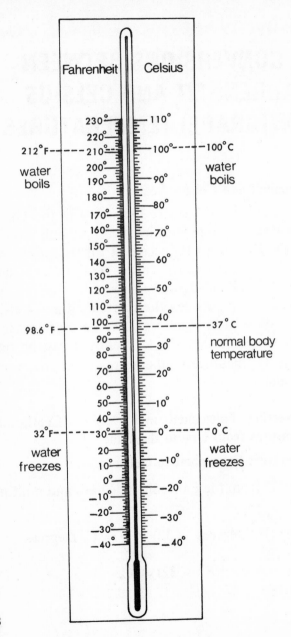

Fig. 5-1. Fahrenheit and Celsius Scales.

58

Example (1): Convert 32° F. (freezing point of water) to Celsius degrees.

Solution: $(32 - 32) \times \frac{5}{9} = 0 \times \frac{5}{9} = 0°$ C., answer

Example (2): If the temperature of a room is 68° F., what is its Celsius temperature?

Solution: $(68 - 32) \times \frac{5}{9} = \overset{4}{\cancel{36}} \times \frac{5}{\cancel{9}} = 20°$ C., answer

B. To convert Celsius to Fahrenheit:

Multiply the Celsius degrees by 9/5 and add 32.

Formula: (C. Degrees $\times \frac{9}{5}$) + 32 = F. Degrees

$$\frac{9}{5}C. + 32 = F.$$

or: 1.8C. + 32 = F.

Example: (1) Convert 100° C. (boiling point of water) to Fahrenheit degrees.

Solution: $\overset{20}{\cancel{100}} \times \frac{9}{\cancel{5}} = 180; + 32 = 212°$ F., answer

Example (2): If the temperature outdoors is 30° C., what is the Fahrenheit temperature?

Solution: $\overset{6}{\cancel{30}} \times \frac{9}{\cancel{5}} = 54; + 32 = 86°$ F., answer

Table C (page 94) shows the equivalents of temperatures in Fahrenheit and Celsius degrees for various intervals from −40° to 525° Fahrenheit.

5-3. Short-Cut for Approximate Conversion from Fahrenheit to Celsius

To convert F. to approximate C., subtract 30 from the F. degrees and take half of the result.

Example: When the temperature is 38° F., what is the approximate C. temperature?

Short-cut formula: $(F. - 30) \times \frac{1}{2} = $ approx. C.

Approximation: $38 - 30 = 8; \times \frac{1}{2} = 4°$ C. (approx.), answer

Exact conversion: $38 - 32 = 6; \overset{2}{\cancel{6}} \times \frac{5}{\underset{3}{\cancel{9}}} = \frac{10}{3} = 3\frac{1}{3}°$ C.

At 50° F., the approximate and exact conversions give the same result: 10° C. Thus:

Approximation: $50 - 30 = 20; \times \frac{1}{2} = 10°$ C.

Exact conversion: $50 - 32 = 18; \overset{2}{\cancel{18}} \times \frac{5}{\underset{}{\cancel{9}}} = 10°$ C., again.

As temperatures go lower or higher than 50° F., the difference between an exact conversion and an approximate one increases. However, the short-cut gives reasonably accurate results within the range of "living" temperatures. At −10° F., the approximate conversion to C. is 3.3° C. too high, and at 110° F. the conversion is 3.3° C. too low, with smaller differences for all temperatures in between.

VI. METRIC IN THE KITCHEN

6-1. Kitchen Weights and Measures

The approximate equivalents of common kitchen weights and measures in U.S. and metric units are shown in Table 6-1.1. Conversion factors based on these equivalents (and on Table 3-3) are given in Table 6-1.2. (See next 2 pages.)

To use Table 6-1.2, find the known or given unit in the left column and multiply by the conversion factor for the desired unit in the right column. Measuring in metric will require the use of metric cups, liter measures, and metric scales.

Example (1): TEASPOONS to MILLILITERS: If a recipe calls for 2 teaspoons of vinegar, how many milliliters would this be?
Method: Teaspoons × 5 = Milliliters
Solution: 2 tsp. × 5 = 10 ml., answer

Example (2): TABLESPOONS to MILLILITERS: How many milliliters in 3 tablespoons?
Method: Tablespoons × 15 = Milliliters
Solution: 3 tbsp. × 15 = 45 ml., answer

TABLE 6-1.1: APPROXIMATE EQUIVALENTS OF U.S. AND METRIC KITCHEN WEIGHTS AND MEASURES

CAPACITY

Liquid Measure

2 tablespoons (T., Tsp., or tbsp.)	= 1 fluid ounce	= 30 milliliters
1 cup	= 8 fluid ounces	= 0.24 liter (240 ml.)
2 cups	= 1 pint	= 0.47 liter
4 cups	= 1 quart	= 0.95 liter
4 quarts	= 1 gallon	= 3.8 liters

Dry or Liquid Measure

3 teaspoons (t., or tsp.)	= 1 tablespoon	= 15 milliliters
16 tablespoons	= 1 cup	= 0.24 liter

WEIGHT

1 ounce	= 28	grams
$3\frac{1}{2}$ ounces	= 100	grams
16 ounces	= 454	grams
1 pound	= 454	grams
1 pound	= 0.45	kilogram

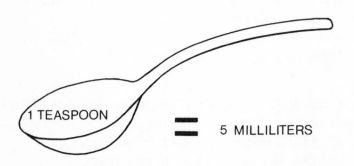

1 TEASPOON = 5 MILLILITERS

TABLE 6-1.2: APPROXIMATE CONVERSION FACTORS: U.S. AND METRIC KITCHEN WEIGHTS AND MEASURES

Teaspoons	×	5	= Milliliters
Tablespoons	×	15	= Milliliters
Fluid Ounces	×	30	= Milliliters
Fluid Ounces	×	0.03	= Liters
Cups	×	240	= Milliliters
Cups	×	0.24	= Liters
Pints	×	0.47	= Liters
Quarts	×	0.95	= Liters
Gallons	×	3.8	= Liters
Ounces	×	28	= Grams
Pounds	×	454	= Grams
Pounds	×	0.45	= Kilograms
Milliliters	×	0.2	= Teaspoons
Milliliters	×	0.07	= Tablespoons
Milliliters	×	0.034	= Fluid Ounces
Liters	×	34	= Fluid Ounces
Milliliters	×	0.004	= Cups
Liters	×	4.2	= Cups
Liters	×	2.1	= Pints
Liters	×	1.06	= Quarts
Liters	×	0.26	= Gallons
Grams	×	0.035	= Ounces
Grams	×	0.002	= Pounds
Kilograms	×	2.2	= Pounds

Small measures, such as "a pinch," "a dash," or "a few drops," should be used without converting; spoons and fractions of spoons may also be so used.

Example (3): CUPS to LITERS: How many liters in 2 cups of flour?

Method: Cups × 0.24 = Liters

Solution: 2 cups × 0.24 = 0.48 l., answer (about ½ liter)

Example (4): OUNCES to GRAMS: How many grams in 4 ounces (¼ lb.) of butter?

Method: Ounces × 28 = Grams

Solution: 4 oz. × 28 = 112 g., answer

6-2. Converting Oven Temperatures from Fahrenheit to Celsius

The formula for converting from Fahrenheit to Celsius (and Celsius to Fahrenheit) is given in Section 5-2. Equivalents of oven temperatures in Fahrenheit and Celsius degrees up to 525° F. are included in Table C (page 94).

6-3. Converting Cooking Time Per Pound to Time Per Kilogram

Example (1): If a turkey is to be roasted at 350° F. (177° C.) for 25 minutes per pound, how long should it be cooked per kilogram?

Method: Cooking Time per Pound × 2.2 = Cooking Time per Kilogram

Solution: 25 min. per lb. × 2.2 = 55 min. per kg., answer

Example (2): A smoked ham is to be boiled for 20 minutes per pound. How long per kilogram?

Solution: 20 min. per lb. × 2.2 = 44 min. per kg., answer

6-4. Counting Calories in Metric

Calories (Cal.) per ounce, tablespoon, cup, or fluid ounce may be converted to metric units as follows.

A. To convert calories per ounce to calories per gram:

Example: There are about 100 calories per ounce in Swiss cheese. How many calories per gram would this be?

Method: Calories per Ounce × 0.035 = Calories per Gram

Solution: 100 Cal. per oz. × 0.035 = 3.5 Cal. per g., answer

B. To convert calories per tablespoon to calories per milliliter:

Example: In a tablespoon of mayonnaise, there are about 100 calories. How many calories per milliliter?

Method: Calories per Tablespoon × 0.07 = Calories per Milliliter

Solution: 100 Cal. × 0.07 = 7 Cal. per ml., answer

C. To convert calories per cup to calories per liter:

Example: There are about 160 calories in a cup (8 fl. oz.) of whole milk. How many calories per liter?

Method: Calories per Cup × 4.2 = Calories per Liter

Solution: 160 Cal. per cup × 4.2 = 672 Cal. per l., answer

D. To convert calories per fluid ounce to calories per milliliter:

Example: If there are 20 calories per fluid ounce in a beverage, how many calories are there per milliliter?

Method: Calories per Fluid Ounce × 0.034 = Calories per Milliliter

Solution: 20 Cal. per fl. oz. × 0.034 = 0.68 Cal. per ml., answer

6-5. Calories and Your Weight

The calorie, the unit used for measuring the heat energy a food or beverage can supply to the body, is really a kilocalorie, although commonly called simply a "calorie."

In U.S. units, if you "take in" 3,500 more calories than you "use up," you will gain about a pound, and this added weight will be stored in the body as fat. To lose a pound of this fat, you must use up 3,500 more calories than you take in. If you are watching your weight in kilograms, these calories should be calculated at the rate of 7,700 per kilogram instead of 3,500 per pound.

VII. METRIC AND THE CAR

Again, the conversions in this chapter are based on the approximate conversion factors of Table 3-3. Measuring speeds and distances in metric will require a speedometer calibrated in kilometers.

7-1. Converting Miles to Kilometers

Example (1): If a car is driven 400 miles, how far would this be in kilometers?
Method: Miles × 1.6 = Kilometers
Solution: 400 mi. × 1.6 = 640 km., answer

Example (2): If you drive for 3 hours and average 50 miles per hour (mph), how far would you go in kilometers?
Formula: Rate of Speed × Time = Distance
Solution:
(a) 50 mph × 3 (hr.) = 150 mi. travelled
(b) 150 mi. × 1.6 = 240 km., answer

Table 7-1 gives approximate conversion factors that may be used in conversions between miles and kilometers, gallons and liters, and miles per gallon and kilometers per liter.   (See next page.)

TABLE 7-1: APPROXIMATE CONVERSION FACTORS: MILES AND KILOMETERS; GALLONS AND LITERS: MILES PER GALLON AND KILOMETERS PER LITER

Miles	$\times 1.6$	= Kilometers
Gallons	$\times 3.8$	= Liters
Miles per gallon	$\times 0.42$	= Kilometers per liter
Kilometers	$\times 0.62$	= Miles
Liters	$\times 0.26$	= Gallons
Kilometers per liter	$\times 2.4$	= Miles per gallon

$\dfrac{\text{Miles}}{\text{Gallons}} = $ Miles Per Gallon; $\times 0.42 = $ Kilometers Per Liter

$\dfrac{\text{Kilometers}}{\text{Liters}} = $ Kilometers Per Liter; $\times 2.4 = $ Miles Per Gallon

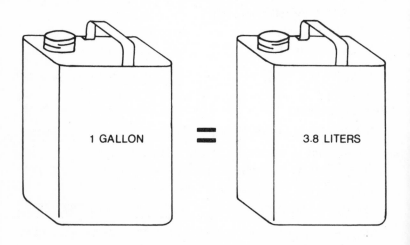

1 GALLON = 3.8 LITERS

7-2. Converting Miles Per Gallon to Kilometers Per Liter

Example: If a car goes 12 miles per gallon of gasoline, how many kilometers does it go per liter?

Method: Miles per gallon × 0.42 = Kilometers per Liter

Solution: 12 mi. per gal. × 0.42 = 5.04 km. per l., answer

7-3. Computing Kilometers Per Liter

Example: If a car goes 1,600 kilometers on 250 liters of gasoline, how many kilometers does it go per liter?

Formula: $\dfrac{\text{Kilometers}}{\text{Liters}}$ = Kilometers per Liter

Solution: $\dfrac{\overset{32}{\cancel{1600}}\text{ km.}}{\underset{5}{\cancel{250}}\text{ l.}} = \dfrac{32}{5} = 6.4$ km. per l., answer

In miles per gallon: 6.4 km. per l. × 2.4 = 15.36 mi. per gal.

7-4. Converting Miles Per Hour to Kilometers Per Hour

Example (1): If a car is going 60 miles per hour (mph), what is its speed in kilometers per hour?

Method: Miles per Hour × 1.6 = Kilometers per hour

Solution: 60 mph × 1.6 = 96 km. per hr., answer

Example (2): If the speed limit on a road is 50 miles an hour, what is the limit in kilometers per hour?

Solution: 50 mph × 1.6 = 80 km. per hr., answer

7-5. Converting Cost Per Mile to Cost Per Kilometer

Example: If it cost $1,500 to operate a car for 10,000 miles, what was the cost per mile and per kilometer?

Formula: $\dfrac{\text{Cost of Operating Car}}{\text{Miles Travelled}} = \text{Cost per Mile}$

$\text{Cost per Mile} \times 0.62 = \text{Cost per Kilometer}$

Solution:

(a) $\dfrac{\$15\cancel{0}\cancel{0}}{10\cancel{0}\cancel{0}\cancel{0} \text{ mi.}} = \$.15$, cost per mi.

(b) $.15 per mi. $\times$ 0.62 = $.093, cost per km., answer
also: 10,000 mi. $\times$ 1.6 = 16,000 km.; $1,500 ÷ 16,000
km. = $.093 per km., again

7-6. Converting Stopping Distance in Feet to Distance in Meters

Example: If it takes 200 feet to stop a certain car going 60 miles an hour, what is the stopping distance in meters?

Method: Feet $\times$ 0.3 = Meters
Solution: 200 ft. $\times$ 0.3 = 60 m., answer

7-7. Converting Piston Displacement in Cubic Inches to Displacement in Cubic Centimeters

Example: If the piston displacement (cubic displacement) of an engine is 300 cubic inches, what is the displacement in cubic centimeters (cc)?

Method: Cubic Inches $\times$ 16.4 = Cubic Centimeters
Solution: 300 cu. in. $\times$ 16.4 = 4,920 cc (or 4,920 cm.³),
answer (= 4.92 liters)

7-8. Converting Tire Pressure in Pounds Per Square Inch to Kilograms (or Grams) Per Square Centimeter

Example: If the air pressure in a tire is 25 pounds (per square inch), what is the pressure in kilograms per square centimeter?

Method: Pounds per Square Inch × 0.07 = Kilograms per Square Centimeter

Solution: 25 lb. per sq. in. × 0.07 = 1.75 kg. per cm.^{2}, answer

or:

25 lb. per sq. in. × 70 = 1,750 grams per cm.^{2}

VIII. SHORT-CUT CONVERSIONS FROM U.S. TO METRIC

A short-cut can save time and work in computation, is useful for making quick estimates, and provides a handy way to check an answer or to estimate an answer in advance. The short-cuts in this chapter may be used for any of these purposes.

8-1. Converting Inches to Millimeters and Centimeters

A. To convert inches to millimeters:

Divide inches by 4 and multiply by 100.

Example: Convert 46 inches to millimeters.

Short-cut: 46 (in.) ÷ 4 = 11.5; × 100 = 1,150 mm., answer

same as: 46 in.

              × 25 (conversion factor, in. to mm.)
              ─────
              230

              92
              ─────
             1150 mm.

B. To convert inches to centimeters:

Divide inches by 4 and multiply by 10.

Example: How many centimeters in 53 inches?

Short-cut: 53 (in.) ÷ 4 = 13.25; × 10 = 132.5 cm., answer

same as: 53 in.
      × 2.5 (conversion factor, in. to cm.)

      265
      106

      132.5 cm.

8-2. Converting Yards to Meters

To convert yards to meters, subtract 1/10 (0.1) of the yards from the yards.

Example: How many meters in 138 yards?

Short-cut: 138.0 yd.
      − 13.8

      124.2 m., answer

same as: 138 yd.
      × .9 (conversion factor, yd. to m.)

      124.2 m.

8-3. Converting Miles to Kilometers

If the number of miles is divisible by 5 (the number ends in 5 or 0), it is easy to convert to kilometers by multiplying miles by 8/5.

Example: Convert 125 miles to kilometers.

Short-cut: $\overset{25}{\cancel{125}}$ mi. $\times \dfrac{8}{\cancel{5}} = 200$ km., answer

same as: 125 mi.
      × 1.6 (conversion factor, mi. to km.)

      750
      125

      200.0 km.

8-4. Converting Square Miles to Square Kilometers

To convert square miles to square kilometers, divide square miles by 4 and multiply by 10.

Example: About how many square kilometers are there in 34 square miles?

Short-cut: 34 (sq. mi.) ÷ 4 = 8.5; × 10 = 85 km.^{2}, answer

almost the same as:

$$34 \text{ sq. mi.}$$
$$\underline{\times\ 2.6} \text{ (conversion factor, sq. mi.}$$
$$204 \qquad\qquad \text{to km.}^2)$$
$$\underline{68}$$
$$88.4 \text{ km.}^2$$

The short-cut gives a result about 4% less than that obtained by using the conversion factor, 2.6.

8-5. Converting Cubic Inches to Cubic Centimeters

Example: If an engine has a piston displacement of 276 cubic inches, what is its displacement in cubic centimeters?

Short-cut: Divide cubic inches by 6 and attach two zeros:

276 (cu. in.) ÷ 6 = 46; attach two zeros:

4,600 cm.^{3}, or 4,600 cc, answer (= 4.6 liters)

almost the same as:

$$276 \text{ cu. in.}$$
$$\underline{\times\ 16.4} \text{ (conversion factor, cu. in. to cm.}^3)$$
$$1104$$
$$1656$$
$$\underline{276}$$
$$4526.4 \text{ cm.}^3 \text{ (or cc)}$$

The short-cut gives a result 1.6% greater than that obtained by using the conversion factor, 16.4.

8-6. Converting Cubic Yards to Cubic Meters

To convert cubic yards to cubic meters, multiply cubic yards by 3/4.

Example: About how many cubic meters in 136 cubic yards?

Short-cut: $\overset{34}{\cancel{136}}$ (cu. yd.) $\times \dfrac{3}{\cancel{4}} = 102$ m.³, answer

     almost the same as:

       136 cu. yd.

      $\times$ .76 (conversion factor, cu. yd. to m.³)

       816

      952

   103.36 m.³

The short-cut gives a result 1.3% less than that obtained by using the conversion factor, 0.76.

8-7. Converting Pounds to Kilograms

To convert pounds to kilograms, divide pounds by 2 and subtract 1/10 (0.1) of the result.

Example: How many kilograms in 18 pounds?

Short-cut: 18 (lb.) $\div 2 = 9$; $- 0.9 = 8.1$ kg., answer

same as: 18 lb.

      $\times$ .45 (conversion factor, lb. to kg.)

      90

      72

   8.10 kg.

For a short-cut conversion of Fahrenheit degrees to Celsius (centigrade), see Section 5-3.

IX. WORKING WITH METRIC MEASUREMENTS

9-1. Some Basics of Measurement

Measuring is a process of *comparing*. When we measure a length, for example, we compare the length we are measuring with a length we *know*—that of a ruler, tape measure, or other measuring device. We then express the result in a "unit of measure," such as in meters, or parts of meters.

A *unit of measure* is a precisely defined quantity that can be used for measuring other quantities of the same kind, such as the meter for measuring length, the kilogram for mass (weight), and the liter for volume. A *standard of measure* is a unit in physical form—an object that can be employed to measure other objects.

Suppose, for example, we could make a metal rod the length of a meter, as it is precisely defined. We would then have a "standard" meter—a meter in physical existence. Meter sticks and tape measures may be compared with such a "standard" as a check on their "accuracy."

The "standard" kilogram actually *is* a metal cylinder kept by the International Bureau of Weights and Measures at Paris. There are standards for other units, too, and such standards are duplicated, more or less accurately, in our measuring devices. The closer a device is made to its standard, the more "accurate" it is said to be.

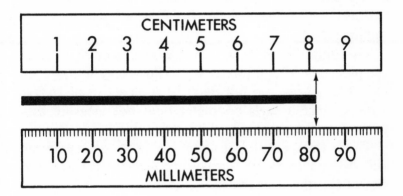

9-2. Precision in Measurement

In measurement, *precision* refers to the *unit of measure* —to the *size* of the unit used. The smaller this unit is, the more precise the measurement.

For example, if we measure a length with a ruler calibrated only in centimeters, we can measure the length only to the nearest centimeter. The unit used is 1 centimeter, and the precision is said to be 1 centimeter, also. If the length we are measuring falls *between* two marks on the ruler, we can only guess or estimate what part of a centimeter this is.

However, if we use a ruler marked in *millimeters*, we can then measure to the nearest millimeter—to a precision of 1 millimeter—and the measurement will be more precise because of the smaller unit used.

But a measurement can't be made more precise by merely stating the result using smaller units. A length measured in centimeters, such as 40 centimeters, can *not* be made more precise by calling it "400 millimeters," because the measurement itself was not made in millimeters.

The unit shown in a measurement should indicate the precision. If you travelled 16 kilometers in a car, for example, you would not describe it as a trip of 16,000 meters, since a car's odometer does not measure distance with the precision of 1 meter.

Thus, the precision obtainable in a measurement will depend upon the measuring device used and the size of the unit it provides.

9-3. Computation with Measurement Numbers

A. If the units of measurement numbers are alike, the numbers themselves may be added, subtracted, multiplied, and divided in the usual way, with units in the answers as shown.

Addition: 6 cm. $+$ 9 cm. $=$ 15 *centimeters* (cm.)

Subtraction: 7 m. $-$ 4 m. $=$ 3 *meters* (m.)

Multiplication: 5 mm. $\times$ 6 $=$ 30 *millimeters* (mm.)
4 m. $\times$ 7 m. $=$ 28 *square meters* (m.²)
5 cm. $\times$ 6 cm. $\times$ 2 cm. $=$ 60 *cubic centimeters* (cm.³)

Division: 24 mm. ÷ 6 = 4 *millimeters* (mm.)

$$\frac{\overset{3}{\cancel{6}}\ \cancel{l.}}{\cancel{2}\ \cancel{l.}} = 3$$

(6 liters contain 2 liters three times; notice how the units "cancel" each other here and in the next two examples)

$$\frac{\overset{2}{\cancel{6}}\ \cancel{mm.} \times 4\ \text{mm.}}{\cancel{3}\ \cancel{mm.}} = 8\ \textit{millimeters}\ (\text{mm.})$$

$$\frac{\overset{8}{\cancel{24}}\ \text{cm.}\cancel{^2}}{\cancel{3}\ \cancel{cm.}} = 8\ \textit{centimeters}\ (\text{cm.})$$

B. If the units of measurement numbers are not alike, the units must be changed to be alike before computing with them.

Example (1): Add a length of 12 centimeters to a length of 3 meters.

Solution: Change 12 cm. to 0.12 m. and add *meters:* 0.12 m. + 3 m. = 3.12 meters, answer

or: Change 3 m. to 300 cm. and add *centimeters:* 12 cm. + 300 cm. = 312 centimeters, answer

Example (2): If you have 1 liter of water and pour off 150 milliliters, how much water remains in the liter?

Solution: Change 1 liter to 1,000 milliliters and subtract *milliliters:*

1,000 ml. − 150 ml. = 850 milliliters, answer

9-4. Rounding Off Measurements

Rounding off measurements can often simplify computation and enable you to make quick estimates.

A *whole number* is rounded by dropping one or more digits on the right and substituting a zero or zeros. If a dropped digit is 5 or more, the next remaining digit on the left is increased by 1.

Example: A distance of 2,637 kilometers (measured to the nearest kilometer on a car's odometer) may be rounded:

To the nearest ten kilometers: 2,640
To the nearest hundred kilometers: 2,600
To the nearest thousand kilometers: 3,000

A *decimal number* is rounded by dropping one or more digits to the right of the decimal point. Again, if a dropped digit is 5 or more, the next remaining digit on the left is increased by 1.

Example: A length of 2.183 meters (measured to the nearest thousandth of a meter, or nearest millimeter) may be rounded:

To the nearest hundredth of a meter: 2.18
To the nearest tenth of a meter: 2.2
To the nearest whole meter: 2

A. Rounding for making an estimate:

Sometimes a good estimate or approximation may be all you need and can save a lot of needless figuring.

Example: If a wall is 2.7 meters high and 4.3 meters long, its area in square meters (Height × Length) may be estimated as follows.

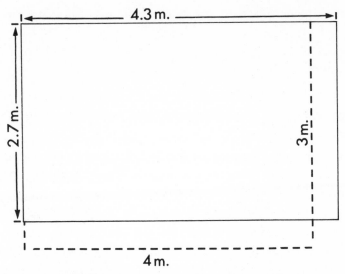

(Broken lines show effect of rounding)

Estimate: Round 2.7 m. to 3 m.; round 4.3 m. to 4 m., then multiply: 3 m. × 4 m. = 12 m.², estimated area

Multiplying the measurements themselves, 2.7 m. × 4.3 m., will give the product 11.61 m.². This is close enough to the estimate to show that at least no *big* mistake was made in multiplying 2.7 by 4.3. The estimate thus also provides a check on the answer.

When rounding two measurements for multiplication, increasing one number and decreasing the other like this will give a better estimate than if both numbers are increased or decreased. For example, if 2.7 and 4.3

are both increased to the next whole numbers, we have $3 \times 5 = 15$; if both are decreased, we get $2 \times 4 = 8$. Neither result is as close to the actual product (11.61) as obtained with $3 \times 4 = 12$.

B. Rounding of conversion factors:

Conversion factors given in tables are often more accurate (have more digits) than required for everyday use. The factor for converting centimeters to inches, for example, may be given as 0.3937. If used to convert a measurement such as 5 centimeters to inches, we get 5 cm. $\times$ 0.3937 = 1.9685 in. In the conversion, the precision of 1 cm. (in 5 cm.) has been changed to 0.0001 in. (in 1.9685 in.) which is much more precise than justified by the original measurement. Rounding the converted measurement to 2 in. gives a better result.

Of course, the factor itself (0.3937) may be rounded to 0.4, so that we get 5 cm. $\times$ 0.4 = 2 in., again. The factor, 0.4, is sufficiently accurate for everyday use and greatly simplifies the conversion. The conversion factors in this book have been rounded this way for easy application.

X. SIMPLE SCIENCE IN METRIC

10-1. Relationship Between Weight and Volume—Water

In the U.S. system, a fluid ounce of water weighs about an ounce avoirdupois, a pint about a pound, and a quart about 2 pounds. For small amounts of water, this provides a handy basis for quickly estimating the weight of water from its volume, or the other way around. For larger amounts, however, the conversions become more difficult. A gallon of water, for instance, weighs 8.34 pounds, so gallons must be multiplied by 8.34 to convert them to pounds.

In the metric system, things are much easier. The standard kilogram was made to equal the mass (weight) of 1 cubic decimeter of water at 4° C., so each cubic decimeter (or liter) of water weighs 1 kilogram; each cubic centimeter (or milliliter) weighs 1 gram; and 1 cubic meter of water weighs 1 metric ton. This simple volume-weight relationship is of practical value since any weight of water may be easily converted to its volume, and vice versa.

Table 10-1 shows the weight of water in relation to volume in metric and U.S. units. Note that 1 unit of metric volume equals 1 unit of metric weight for units that are on the same line in the table. Therefore, the number of volume units will always equal the number of weight units, if the units are correctly matched.

TABLE 10-1: WEIGHT OF WATER IN RELATION TO VOLUME IN METRIC AND U.S. UNITS

Volume	Weight
Metric Units	
1 cubic centimeter	1 gram
1 milliliter	1 gram
1 cubic decimeter (1,000 cm.³)	1 kilogram
1 liter (1,000 ml., or 1 dm.³)	1 kilogram
1 cubic meter (1,000 liters)	1 metric ton (1,000 kg.)
U.S. Units	
1 cubic inch	0.058 ounce
1 cubic foot (1,728 cu.in.)	62.4 pounds
1 quart (57.75 cu.in.; 32 fl.oz.)	2.09 pounds
1 gallon (231 cu.in.)	8.34 pounds

Example (1): If an aquarium has 75 liters (about 20 gal.) of water in it, how much does the water weigh?

Solution: 75 l. of water weigh 75 kg. (about 165 lb.), answer

Example (2): If a quantity of water weighs 210 grams, what is its volume in milliliters?

Solution: 210 g. of water have a volume of 210 ml., answer

Other examples

12 cubic centimeters of water weigh 12 grams.

2 kilograms of water have a volume of 2 cubic decimeters (or 2 liters).

3 cubic meters of water weigh 3 metric tons.

10-2. Weights of Other Common Substances

The weights of substances other than water are easily found from their volumes if their "densities" are known. The *density* of a substance is its mass (weight) in relation to its volume, as in the following formulas.

$$Formula: \frac{\text{Grams of a Substance}}{\text{Cubic Centimeters of the Substance}} = \begin{array}{l} \text{Density} \\ \text{(of substance)} \end{array}$$

$$or: \frac{\text{Kilograms of a Substance}}{\text{Liters of the Substance}} = \text{Density}$$

The density of water is 1 since 1 gram of water has a volume of 1 cubic centimeter (or 1 milliliter), and 1 kilogram of water has a volume of 1 cubic decimeter (or 1 liter). A substance with a density of 2 is twice as "heavy" as water, one with a density of 3 is three times as heavy as water, and so on. Densities of some common substances are shown in Table 10-2.

A substance with a density of less than 1 will float in water (fresh), but anything with a density of more than 1 will sink. Ice has a density of 0.92, so, of course, it floats. Sea water has a density of 1.03 and is therefore more buoyant (easier to float in) than fresh water.

TABLE 10-2: DENSITIES OF SOME COMMON SUBSTANCES

(density can vary according to composition and processing)

	Density		Density
Aluminum	2.7	Mercury	13.6
Brass	8.5	Nickel	8.8
Brick (common)	1.8	Oil (lubricating)	0.88
Coal (hard)	1.5	Platinum	21.5
Concrete	2.4	Sand (dry)	2.4
Copper	8.9	Silver	10.5
Cork	0.24	Steel	7.8
Diamond	3.3	Tin	7.2
Earth (loose)	1.2	Water (fresh)	1.0
Gasoline	0.67	Water (sea)	1.03
Glass (common)	2.6	Wood: Maple	0.74
Gold	19.3	Oak (red)	0.74
Ice	0.92	Pine (yellow)	0.59
Iron	7.8	Walnut	0.66
Lead	11.4	Zinc	7.1

Conversion Factors

Density $\times$ 62.4 = Pounds per cubic foot

Pounds per cubic foot $\times$ 0.016 = Density

A. To find the weight of a substance when its volume and density are known:

Example (1): If a bag holds 10 liters of sand, how much would the sand weigh?

Formula: Volume (in liters) $\times$ Density = Weight (in kilograms)

Solution: From Table 10-2, the density of sand is 2.4 (it weighs 2.4 kg. per liter):

10 1. × 2.4 = 24 kg., weight of sand, answer

Example (2): If a barrel holds 160 liters (about 42 gal.) of lubricating oil, how much would the oil weigh?

Solution: From Table 10-2, the density of oil is 0.88:

160 1. × 0.88 = 140.8 kg. (about 310 lb.), answer

B. To find the volume of a substance when its weight and density are known:

Example (1): If a bag of granulated sugar weighs 1 kilogram, about how many liters would this be?

Formula: $\dfrac{\text{Weight (in kilograms)}}{\text{Density}}$ = Volume (in liters)

The weight/volume ratio of dry granulated sugar is about 0.85 and this may be used as a "density" in problems like this one.

Solution: $\dfrac{1 \text{ kg.}}{0.85}$ = almost 1.2 liters of sugar, answer

If the 1.2 liters (1,200 milliliters) are measured into metric cups of 250 milliliters each, we have almost 5 cups (4.8) of sugar per kilogram, and each cup would weigh a little over 200 grams.

Example (2): If you order a metric ton of earth (loose dirt) for the yard, about how many cubic meters should you expect to get?

Formula: $\dfrac{\text{Weight (in tons)}}{\text{Density}} = \text{Volume (in cubic meters)}$

Solution: From Table 10-2, earth has a density of 1.2:

$$\frac{1 \text{ ton}}{1.2} = 0.83 \text{ cubic meter of earth, answer}$$

In the U.S. system, the weights of substances are sometimes given in pounds per cubic foot. To convert between densities and pounds per cubic foot, the factors at the bottom of Table 10-2 may be used.

Example: How many pounds would a cubic foot of ice weigh?

Formula: Density $\times$ 62.4 = Pounds Per Cubic Foot

Solution: From Table 10-2, the density of ice is 0.92:

$$0.92 \times 62.4 = 57.4 \text{ lb. (in 1 cu. ft.), answer}$$

10-3. Work and Power

In U.S. units, *work* is generally measured in "foot-pounds." A *foot-pound* (ft.-lb.) equals the work done in lifting 1 pound up 1 foot. For example, if you lift a 10-pound weight 5 feet up, you do 10 (lb.) $\times$ 5 (ft.) = 50 ft.-lb. of work.

Power is the *rate* of doing work. The faster the work is done, the more power is expended. A *horsepower* (h.p.) is equal to 550 ft.-lb. of work per second (or 33,000 ft.-lb. per minute). This unit was originally derived by measuring the rate at which a strong horse could do work.

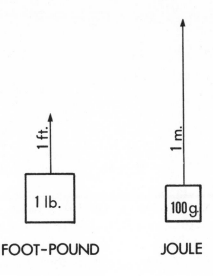

FOOT-POUND   **JOULE**

Formula: $\dfrac{\text{Foot-Pounds}}{\text{Seconds} \times 550} = \text{Horsepower}$

Example: If a man weighing 160 pounds walks up a flight of stairs 10 feet high in 8 seconds, about how much horsepower does he use?

Solution: $\dfrac{\overset{2}{\cancel{10}} \text{ (ft.)} \times \overset{2}{\cancel{160}} \text{ (lb.)}}{\underset{11}{\cancel{8} \text{ (sec.)} \times \cancel{550}}} = \dfrac{4}{11}$, or about $\dfrac{1}{3}$ h.p.,

answer

In the metric system, the basic unit of work (as well as heat) is the *joule* (J), and the unit of power is the *watt* (W). A watt is equal to 1 joule per second. These are small units. If you lift a small-size potato (about 100 grams) 1 meter up, that would be about 1 joule of work;

if you do it in 1 second, you have expended 1 watt of power.

The watt, of course, is the same unit we have long used for measuring electrical power. In the metric system, the watt is used for mechanical power, too, so that a separate unit like "horsepower" is not needed. Other electrical units that are the same in the U.S. and metric systems include the *ampere*, used to measure the quantity of current flowing, and the *volt*, the unit of electrical "potential" or "pressure."

Various U.S. and metric units of energy, work, and power may be converted from one to another by means of the factors in Table 10-3. For example, the man who used $\frac{1}{3}$ horsepower in going up the stairs expended $\frac{1}{3} \times 746$ watts, or about 250 W. An engine that develops 100 horsepower would develop $100 \times 746 = 74,600$ watts, or 74.6 kilowatts.

TABLE 10-3: CONVERSION FACTORS: FOOT-POUNDS, JOULES, WATTS, AND HORSEPOWER

Foot-pounds	×	1.36	= Joules
Joules	×	0.74	= Foot-pounds
Joules per second	×	1	= Watts
Watts	×	1	= Joules per second
Watts	×	0.001	= Kilowatts
Kilowatts	×	1,000	= Watts
Horsepower	×	746	= Watts
Horsepower	×	0.746	= Kilowatts
Watts	×	0.00134	= Horsepower
Kilowatts	×	1.34	= Horsepower

Bills for electricity are based upon the number of kilowatt-hours used, as measured by the power company's electric meter. The number of watts used, times the number of hours, equals watt-hours; dividing this by 1,000 gives kilowatt-hours.

Formula: $\dfrac{\text{Watts} \times \text{Hours}}{1000} = \text{Kilowatt-Hours}$

Example: If an electric heater uses 1,300 watts and is "on" for 4 hours a day, how many kilowatt-hours would this be per day?

Solution: $\dfrac{\overset{1.3}{\cancel{1300}}\,(W) \times 4\,(hr.)}{\cancel{1000}} = 5.2$ kilowatt-hours per day, answer

The wattage rating of an electrical appliance is generally shown on the device, but you may have to look hard to find it. Sometimes the information is shown as "amperes" and "volts," in which case you can calculate the wattage by the formula: Amperes × Volts = Watts.

TABLE A: APPROXIMATE EQUIVALENTS OF U.S. AND METRIC DISTANCES COMMONLY USED IN SPORTS EVENTS

Based on 1 yard = 0.91 meter, and 1 meter = 1.1 yard

50 yards	=	45 meters
100 yards	=	91 meters
220 yards ($\frac{1}{8}$ mi.)	=	200 meters
440 yards ($\frac{1}{4}$ mi.)	=	400 meters
880 yards ($\frac{1}{2}$ mi.)	=	800 meters
1 mile	=	1,600 meters (1.6 km.)
$1\frac{1}{8}$ miles	=	1,800 meters (1.8 km.)
$1\frac{1}{4}$ miles	=	2,000 meters (2 km.)
$1\frac{1}{2}$ miles	=	2,400 meters (2.4 km.)
2 miles	=	3,200 meters (3.2 km.)
3 miles	=	4,800 meters (4.8 km.)
4 miles	=	6,400 meters (6.4 km.)
5 miles	=	8,000 meters (8 km.)
6 miles	=	9,600 meters (9.6 km.)
10 miles	=	16,000 meters (16 km.)
500 miles	=	800 kilometers
60 meters	=	66 yards
80 meters	=	88 yards
100 meters	=	110 yards ($\frac{1}{16}$ mi.)
110 meters	=	121 yards
200 meters	=	220 yards ($\frac{1}{8}$ mi.)
400 meters	=	440 yards ($\frac{1}{4}$ mi.)
800 meters	=	880 yards ($\frac{1}{2}$ mi.)
1,200 meters	=	1,320 yards ($\frac{3}{4}$ mi.)
1,500 meters	=	1,650 yards ($\frac{15}{16}$ mi.)
1,600 meters	=	1,760 yards (1 mi.)
2,400 meters	=	2,640 yards ($1\frac{1}{2}$ mi.)
2,500 meters	=	2,750 yards ($1\frac{9}{16}$ mi.)
3,000 meters	=	3,300 yards ($1\frac{7}{8}$ mi.)

```
 4,000 meters      =  4,400 yards (2½ mi.)
 5,000 meters      =  5,500 yards (3⅛ mi.)
10,000 meters      = 11,000 yards (6¼ mi.)
20,000 meters      = 22,000 yards (12½ mi.)
```

1 furlong =   220 yards = ⅛ mile =   200 meters
2 furlongs =   440 yards = ¼ mile =   400 meters
3 furlongs =   660 yards = ⅜ mile =   600 meters
4 furlongs =   880 yards = ½ mile =   800 meters
5 furlongs = 1,100 yards = ⅝ mile = 1,000 meters
6 furlongs = 1,320 yards = ¾ mile = 1,200 meters
7 furlongs = 1,540 yards = ⅞ mile = 1,400 meters
8 furlongs = 1,760 yards = 1 mile = 1,600 meters

(1 furlong = exactly 201.168 meters)

TABLE B: FRACTIONS OF AN INCH BY THIRTY-SECONDS AND EQUIVALENTS IN MILLIMETERS

1 inch = 25.4 millimeters (exactly)

Inch	Millimeters	Inch	Millimeters
$\frac{1}{32}$	0.79	$\frac{17}{32}$	13.49
$\frac{1}{16}$	1.59	$\frac{9}{16}$	14.29
$\frac{3}{32}$	2.38	$\frac{19}{32}$	15.08
$\frac{1}{8}$	3.18	$\frac{5}{8}$	15.88
$\frac{5}{32}$	3.97	$\frac{21}{32}$	16.67
$\frac{3}{16}$	4.76	$\frac{11}{16}$	17.46
$\frac{7}{32}$	5.56	$\frac{23}{32}$	18.26
$\frac{1}{4}$	6.35	$\frac{3}{4}$	19.05
$\frac{9}{32}$	7.14	$\frac{25}{32}$	19.84
$\frac{5}{16}$	7.94	$\frac{13}{16}$	20.64
$\frac{11}{32}$	8.73	$\frac{27}{32}$	21.43
$\frac{3}{8}$	9.53	$\frac{7}{8}$	22.23
$\frac{13}{32}$	10.32	$\frac{29}{32}$	23.02
$\frac{7}{16}$	11.11	$\frac{15}{16}$	23.81
$\frac{15}{32}$	11.91	$\frac{31}{32}$	24.61
$\frac{1}{2}$	12.70	1	25.40 (over)

To change millimeters to centimeters, move the decimal point one place to the left.

Example: $\frac{1}{2}$ in. = 12.7 mm. = 1.27 cm.

TABLE C: EQUIVALENTS IN FAHRENHEIT AND CELSIUS (CENTIGRADE) TEMPERATURES

Celsius temperatures rounded to the nearest tenth of a degree

Degrees Fahrenheit	Degrees Celsius	Degrees Fahrenheit	Degrees Celsius
−40	−40.0	90	32.2
−30	−34.4	95	35.0
−20	−28.9	98.6 body temp.	37.0
−10	−23.3	100	37.8
0	−17.8	110	43.3
5	−15.0	125	51.7
10	−12.2	150	65.6
15	−9.4	175	79.4
20	−6.7	200	93.3
25	−3.9	212 water boils	100.0
30	−1.1	225	107.2
32 water freezes	0	250	121.1
35	1.7	275	135.0
40	4.4	300	148.9
45	7.2	325	162.8
50	10.0	350	176.7
55	12.8	375	190.6
60	15.6	400	204.4
65	18.3	425	218.3
70	21.1	450	232.2
75	23.9	475	246.1
80	26.7	500	260.0
85	29.4	525	273.9

INDEX

acres to hectares, 42, 51
area, in metric, 18, 19-21, 27-28, 31, 42, 45, 49-51
area, in U.S. system, 12, 42, 45, 50-51
avoirdupois weight, 14, 33, 62, 83
bushels to liters, 43, 53
calories, 65-66
capacity, in metric, 20, 31, 43, 45, 53, 62
capacity, in U.S. system, 12, 14, 43, 45, 53, 62
car and metric, 67-71
Celsius scale, 38, 57-60, 64, 94
conversion factors, rounding of, 82
conversion factors, U.S. and metric units, 41-43, 63, 68, 72-75, 82, 90
converting to metric, 36-37, 39-45, 46-56
converting to metric, everyday calculations, 41, 46-56
cooking time, 64-65
cost per mile to cost per kilometer, 70
cubic feet to cubic meters, 43, 52
cubic inches to cubic centimeters, 43, 52, 74
cubic yards to cubic meters, 43, 52, 75
cups to liters, 63, 64
decimal system, 7, 17, 19
density, 85-88
distances, sports, 92-93
dry measure, metric, 43, 62
dry measure, U.S., 12, 43, 62
electrical power units, 90-91
English system of weights and measures, 6
Fahrenheit scale, 57-60, 64, 94
feet and inches to centimeters, 47
feet to centimeters, 42, 46
feet to meters, 42, 48
fluid ounces to milliliters, 43, 53
foot-pound, 88-89

fractions of an inch to millimeters, 49, 93
gallons to liters, 43, 53
"going metric," 10-11, 32-45, 39-41
horsepower, 88
inches to centimeters, 42, 46, 72-73
inches to millimeters, 42, 46, 72
International Bureau of Weights and Measures, 8, 77
International Metric System (SI), 30
joule, 89
kilometers per liter, 69
kitchen and metric, 61-66
length, in metric, 18, 31, 42, 44
length, in U.S. system, 12, 42, 44
liquid measure, metric, 20, 43, 62
liquid measure, U.S., 14, 43, 62
measurement, precision in, 77-78
measurement units, early, 5
measuring, definition, 76
meter, definition, 7-8
"metrication" program, 6
metric measurements, working with, 76-82
metric system, basic units, 17
metric system, ease of computation, 32-36
metric system, history of, 6-9
metric units, common, 30-31
miles per gallon to kilometers per liter, 68, 69
miles per hour to kilometers per hour, 69
miles to kilometers, 42, 48, 67-68, 73
National Bureau of Standards, 9
ounces to grams, 43, 53, 64
pints to liters, 43, 53
piston displacement, 70
pound, defined in metric, 9, 17
pounds and ounces to kilograms, 54
pounds to kilograms, 43, 54, 75
power, definition, 88

95

prefixes, metric, 17-19, 26
quarts to liters, 43, 53
rounding off, 40, 80-82
science in metric, 57-60, 83-91, 94
short-cut conversions, U.S. to metric, 72-75
SI, 30
square feet to square meters, 42, 50
square inches to square centimeters, 42, 50
square miles to square kilometers, 42, 51, 74
standard kilogram, 8, 9, 77
standard meter, 8, 9, 76
standard of measure, 76
stopping distance, 70
tablespoons to milliliters, 61-63
teaspoons to milliliters, 61-63
temperature conversions, 57-60, 64, 94
"thinking metric," 36-39
tire pressure, 71
tons to metric tons, 43, 54
unit of measure, 76, 77
unit prices, 55-56
units, metric, conversions within system, 19-30
units, U.S., conversions within system, 14-16

units, U.S. system, 13
U.S.-metric equivalents in whole numbers, 44-45
U.S. Metric Study, 9
U.S. system of weights and measures, 6, 8, 12, 13-16
U.S. system, related to metric, 8-9
volume-capacity-weight relationships of water, metric, 20
volume, in metric, 18, 20, 21, 28, 29, 30, 31, 43, 45, 51-52, 83-88
volume, in U.S. system, 12, 43, 45, 52, 83-86
water, weight-volume relationships, 83-85
watt, 89
weight, in metric, 20, 31, 43, 45, 53-54, 62, 83-88
weight, in U.S., 14, 33, 43, 45, 53-54, 62, 83-85, 88
work and power, 88-91
yard, defined in metric, 9, 17
yards to centimeters, 42, 48
yards to meters, 42, 48, 73

LIST OF TABLES

1-1: U.S. System of Weights and Measures, 12-14

2-1: Metric System of Weights and Measurements, 18-20

2-6: Interrelation of Prefixes for Metric Units of Length, Capacity, and Weight, 26

2-8: Metric Units Commonly Used in Everyday Life, 31

3-3: Approximate Conversion Factors: U.S. and Metric Units, 42

3-4: Approximate Equivalents of Certain U.S. and Metric Units in Whole Numbers, 44

4-7: Approximate Conversions of Unit Prices from U.S. to Metric Units, 55

6-1.1: Approximate Equivalents of U.S. and Metric Kitchen Weights and Measures, 62

6-1.2: Approximate Conversion Factors: U.S. and Metric Kitchen Weights and Measures, 63

7-1: Approximate Conversion Factors: Miles and Kilometers; Gallons and Liters; Miles Per Gallon and Kilometers Per Liter, 68

10-1: Weight of Water in Relation to Volume in Metric and U.S. Units, 84

10-2: Densities of Some Common Substances 86

10-3: Conversion Factors, Foot-Pounds, Joules, Watts, and Horsepower, 90

A: Approximate Equivalents of U.S. and Metric Distances Commonly Used in Sports Events, 92

· B: Fractions of an Inch by Thirty-Seconds and Equivalents in Millimeters, 93

C: Equivalents in Fahrenheit and Celsius (Centigrade) Temperatures, 94